FULL OF
CHARACTER[S]

Promopress is a commercial brand of:
Promotora de prensa internacional S.A.
C/Ausiàs March 124
08013 Barcelona (Spain)
T: (+34) 93 245 14 64
F: (+34) 93 265 48 93
mail: info@promopress.es
www.promopresseditions.com

Editorial project
by Satèl·lit bcn

Editor in chief: Inma Alavedra
Editor: Xènia Gaya
Layout & design: Meri Iannuzzi
CD label design: Promopress
Interview & CD coordination: Agente Morillas
Introduction: Ilu·Station
Spanish translation: Montse Ballesteros
English translation: Hugo Steckelmacher
French translation: François Schapochnikoff
& Sylvie Mathis
Italian translation: Daniel Frisano-Paulon

ISBN: 978-84-92810-35-2
© 2012 PROMOPRESS

First edition: 2012
Printed in China

● Analogue	Analogique	**Analógico**	Analogico
❑ Digital	Digital	**Digital**	Digitale
▲ Sculpture	Sculpture	**Escultura**	Scultura
✤ Puppet / Doll / Toy	Puppet / Doll / Toy	**Puppet / Doll / Toy**	Puppet / Doll / Toy
☆ 3D / Modelling	3D / Modelage	**3D / Modelado**	3D / Modellazione

Illustration is all around us in our daily lives: it can be found in advertising, in the books we read, on the clothes we wear, on the toys we buy, in tattoos, on streets, and in many other places besides. Far removed from established outlets, these new formats expand the creative horizons of illustration, which has traditionally been rooted in two-dimensionality, despite its forays into other more complex supports. These in turn provide unique challenges for artists when it comes to approaching each new project. For instance, some works are only complete when they are reproduced on pieces of clothing or a public wall, when they intervene in the social arena or are viewed in relation to a particular text.

Of these new spaces, one that has proven particularly fertile terrain for the development of illustrators' creativity is mascot design. This type of creation was once exclusively used for the purpose of linking brands with a particular character. However, these characters have since comprehensively outgrown these limitations and are now consumed for their own sake and for their artistic value, regardless of who they represent. People have moved beyond the brands and are now interested in the characters for what they are and

L'illustration fait partie intégrante de notre quotidien, à travers la publicité, les livres que nous lisons, les vêtements que nous portons, les jouets que nous achetons, les tatouages, dans la rue, etc. Ces nouveaux supports, loin du conventionnel, ouvrent davantage de portes à la créativité dans le domaine de l'illustration, traditionnellement installée dans la bi-dimensionnalité, bien que présente dans d'autres supports volumineux. Ceux-ci apportent également leur lot de nouveaux défis aux artistes entamant un nouveau projet. On trouve ainsi des œuvres qui ne voient le jour qu'à travers des reproductions sur des vêtements, des affiches publicitaires, dans un contexte social ou encore, en relation avec un texte.

La conception de mascottes est l'un de ces nouveaux espaces ayant fait office de laboratoire de la créativité pour les illustrateurs. Ce type de création été auparavant utilisé pour établir un lien entre une marque et un personnage concret. Celles-ci prennent désormais des nouvelles dimensions avec des personnages à part entière, possédant une réelle valeur artistique, indépendamment du fait qu'ils représentent ou non quelqu'un ou quelque chose. Les gens, délaissant les marques, s'intéressent davantage aux personnages pour ce qu'ils sont et pour le travail de leur auteur, comme

La ilustración nos rodea en nuestro día a día; está presente en la publicidad, en los libros que leemos, en la ropa que vestimos, en los juguetes que compramos, en los tatuajes, en la calle, etc. Estos nuevos soportes, alejados de lo establecido, amplían las posibilidades creativas de la ilustración, tradicionalmente asentada en la bidimensionalidad, aunque presente en otros soportes con volumen. A su vez, estos aportan nuevos retos para los artistas en el momento de abordar cada proyecto. Así, podemos encontrar obras que solo se completan cuando se reproducen en ropa, en una pared pública, con la intervención del entorno social o en relación a un texto.

Uno de estos nuevos espacios, que ha servido como un gran campo de cultivo para la creatividad de los ilustradores, es el del diseño de mascotas. Antes, este tipo de creaciones se usaba para relacionar una marca con un personaje concreto. Actualmente, esta tendencia se ha visto ampliamente superada, y los personajes se consumen por ellos mismos, por su valor artístico, independientemente de si representan a alguien o no. La gente ha olvidado las marcas y quiere a los personajes por lo que son y por el trabajo de su autor, tal y como podemos comprobar en las dos últimas secciones de este libro. Allí vere-

L'illustrazione è ovunque, nella vita di tutti i giorni: è presente nella pubblicità, nei libri che leggiamo, negli abiti che indossiamo, nei *toys* che acquistiamo, nei tatuaggi, in strada, ecc. Questi nuovi supporti, lontani da schemi fissi, ampliano le possibilità creative dell'illustrazione, tradizionalmente ristretta alla bidimensionalità, seppur presente in altri supporti con volume, e allo stesso tempo propongono nuove sfide agli artisti al momento di affrontare ogni nuovo progetto. Possiamo così trovare opere che si completano solamente una volta riprodotte su un abito, su una parete pubblica, con l'intervento dell'ambiente sociale o in relazione a un testo.

Uno di questi nuovi spazi, che ha svolto la funzione di un grande campo da coltivare per la creatività degli illustratori, è il disegno di mascotte. Se in passato questo tipo di creazione era usato per collegare una marca con un determinato personaggio, questa tendenza si vede ormai ampiamente superata e i personaggi sono oggetto di consumo essi stessi in virtù del loro valore artistico, indipendentemente da chi rappresentano o meno. La gente dimentica la marca e vuole il personaggio per quello che è e per il lavoro de suo autore, come potremo verificare nelle ultime due sezioni di questo libro, dove osserveremo i diversi approcci dei

what they have to say about the artist behind them. This is illustrated in the last two sections of this book, which feature an account of the creative processes embarked on by different artists when setting out to create characters, as well as interviews with four renowned artists in the genre.

This book brings together works by more than one hundred illustrators from all over the world, who stand out for the diversity of their characters and their ability to lend their creations a life of their own. They are ordered by colour, which is the common thread that pervades, structures and delineates the book, providing its conceptual hinge, graphic force and visual unity. This challenging and daring choice is fully in keeping with the spirit of the characters presented in this volume.
We hope you enjoy it.

on pourra le constater dans les deux dernières sections de ce livre. On y verra comment différents artistes abordent la création de personnages à partir de divers processus créatifs et on pourra également lire les réflexions de quatre artistes de renommée avec qui nous nous sommes entretenus.

Ce livre regroupe les travaux de plus d'une centaine d'illustrateurs à travers le monde, se distinguant par leurs personnages variés et pour avoir su doter leurs créations d'une personnalité propre. La palette de couleurs de ces œuvres sert de fil conducteur à l'agencement, la conceptualisation et la différenciation de ce livre, lui conférant unité et force graphique. Un choix difficile et risqué, mais original, en harmonie avec l'esprit des personnages présentés.
Nous espérons que vous apprécierez.

  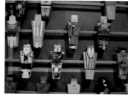

Ilu·Station is a collective made up of five illustrators – two from France, two from Argentina and one from Catalonia. In 2009 they co-founded the Barcelona Independent Illustration and Publishing Festival. They have also organised the children's version of the festival, Mini-Station, and the Golden Globos alternative comic awards, as well as the recent Ilu·Station Workshops.

Ilu·Station est un collectif composé de deux français, deux argentins et un catalan. Ils ont créé ensemble le premier Festival d'Illustration et d'Édition Indépendante de Barcelone en 2009 et sa version destinée aux enfants, la Mini-Station, ainsi que les prix alternatifs de bande dessinée Golden Globos et, plus récemment, les Workshops d'Ilu·Station.

mos cómo diferentes artistas abordan la creación de personajes a partir de distintos procesos creativos y podremos leer las reflexiones de cuatro artistas de renombre a los que hemos entrevistado.

Este libro recoge el trabajo de más de un centenar de ilustradores de todas partes del mundo que destacan por sus personajes variopintos y por haber sabido dotar de personalidad propia a sus creaciones. La gama cromática de las obras es el hilo conductor que atraviesa, organiza, diferencia y conceptualiza su orden en el libro, dándole unidad y fuerza gráfica. Una elección difícil y arriesgada pero original, en sintonía con el espíritu de los personajes presentados.
Esperamos que lo disfrutéis.

vari artisti alla creazione di personaggi partendo da diversi processi creativi e potremo leggere le riflessioni di quattro artisti rinomati da noi intervistati.

Questo libro raccoglie il lavoro di oltre un centinaio di illustratori, provenienti da tutto il mondo, che si distinguono per i loro personaggi variopinti e per aver saputo dotare di personalità propria le loro creazioni. La gamma cromatica delle opere è il filo conduttore che attraversa, organizza, differenzia e concettualizza l'ordine delle stesse nel libro e conferisce loro unità e forza grafica. È stata una scelta difficile e rischiosa ma originale, in sintonia con lo spirito dei personaggi presentati.
Ci auguriamo che vi risulti piacevole.

Ilu·Station es un colectivo formado por dos franceses, dos argentinos y un catalán. Juntos crearon el primer Festival de Ilustración y Edición Independiente de Barcelona en 2009. Asimismo, han organizado la versión infantil del festival, el Mini-Station, así como los premios alternativos de cómic Golden Globos y, recientemente, los Workshops de Ilu·Station.

Ilu·Station è un collettivo formato da due francesi, due argentini e un catalano, che insieme hanno ideato il primo Festival dell'Illustrazione e dell'Edizione Indipendente di Barcellona, nel 2009, oltre a organizzare la versione per bambini del festival, la Mini-Station, i premi alternativi per fumetti Golden Globos e recentemente i Workshop di Ilu·Station.

STANLEY CHOW
N-BOT

FRANK PLANT ▲
THE IDEA

● □ ▲ ♣ ☆

WHERE AM I?

SEBASTIÁN BANDIN ●
AI WEIWEI

the story of my grossesse!

AIIKO VOLSY ● □
MY STORY OF MY GROSSESE

MARK GMEHLING ☆
DRINSCH CHARACTER SERIES

VILLE SAVIMAA ☐
ILLEGAL AFFAIR

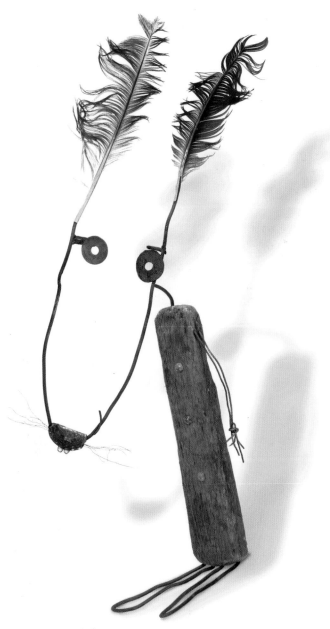

CHRISTIAN VOLTZ ▲
LAPIN

HAPPYMIAOW
MIS MUNDOS, MIS MONSTRUOS

RYAN CHAPMAN
SAILORS

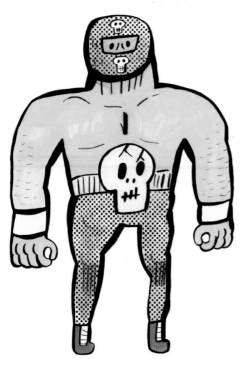

YUSAKU MAEDA ●
THE MAN OF THE GANG OF SKULL

NUMI MIDORI ● ▯
SEÑOR HELADO

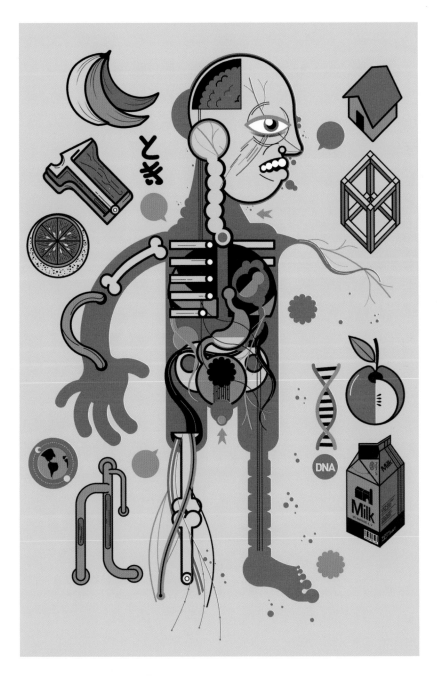

NICOLÁS NAZARENO SARSOTTI □
C.M.Y.K.

HARUKA SHINJI ● □
TWIN SISTERS

HARUKA SHINJI ●
WHITY MICHIYO

LEÓN KITAY ●
BA LIFE – DUALIDAD

GENEVIÈVE GAUCKLER
CORN FISH

● □ ▲ ♣ ☆

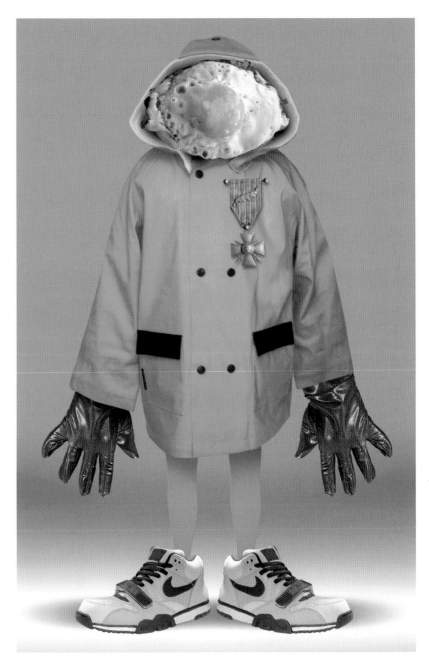

GENEVIÈVE GAUCKLER □
CYCLOP EGG

DIANE KOSS ✤
ROGER

ZEPTONN
BUSINESS CHARACTERS

AGUSTÍN VIGUERA
GROTUS

●□▲♣☆

TUOMAS IKONEN ●□
BE ON TIME

DAN MATUTINA □
BREAKING OUT

BROSMIND (ALEJANDRO & JUAN MINGARRO) ▲
BROSMIND ARMY

● □ ▲ ♣ ☆

MICRO.BARBI ▲
NIÑO VENDA

ISIDRO FERRER ▲
EL CABOLO CUINER

●□▲♣☆

MACN ●□
VOYEUR

ANNA FONT ●
SIN TÍTULO

ISIDRO FERRER
ELEFANTE

WANSAIDE ▢
UNTITLED I

HAPPYMIAOW ✤
TOY

KEITA TAKAHASHI ● ▢
SUNKO

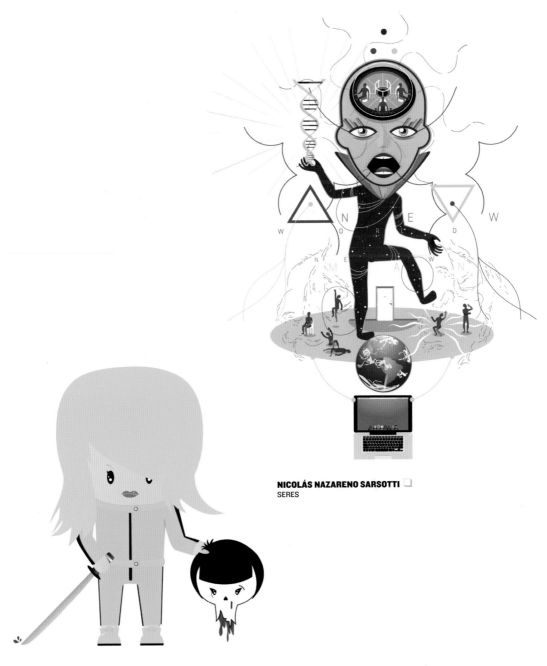

NICOLÁS NAZARENO SARSOTTI
SERES

AGU MÉNDEZ
3.650 DÍAS JUNTOS

PASCAL VALDES
ZEKIDS

RICCARDO ZEMA ☐ ☆
WOODLAND GARDENER

GINA THORSTENSEN ✤
LA EXCURSIONISTA

RICCARDO ZEMA ☆
DOUBLE TROUBLE

SERGIO MORA ● ▢
DOS MALETAS – MARC PARROT

CLÉMENCE KERTUDO ●
DAMA PEZ

JOÃO LAURO FONTE ●☐
THE CAT WHO MISTOOK HIS WHOLE FAMILY FOR A HAT

● □ ▲ ♣ ☆

CHRISTIAN VOLTZ ▲
PERSOMAISON

ISIDRO FERRER ▲
FLAMENCO

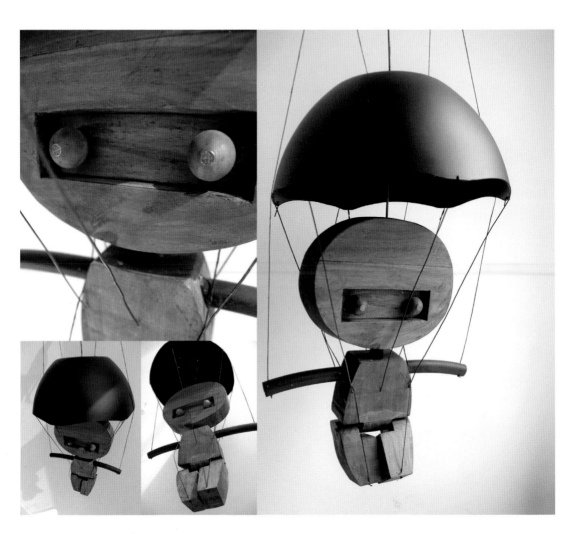

JUAN PABLO CAMBARIERE ✤
SIN TÍTULO

● □ ▲ ♣ ☆

JUAN PABLO CAMBARIERE ♣
SIN TÍTULO

ISIDRO FERRER ▲
LIPAJABRO

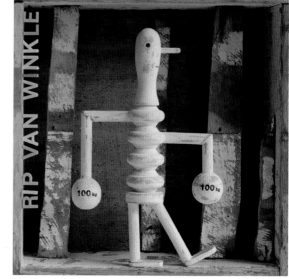

ISIDRO FERRER ▲
RIP VAN WINKLE

●□▲♣☆

RICCARDO ZEMA ☆
ERRANT TIME MACHINE

TECHNO IMAGE - TIAGO HOISEL
AXEL

CHRISTIAN VOLTZ ▲
PINCEAUX

MARK GMEHLING ☆
DRINSCH CHARACTER SERIES

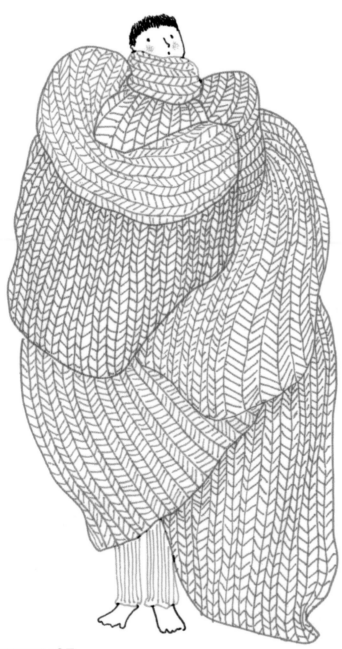

ALICIA VARELA ● ☐
BLANKET

● ▢ ▲ ♣ ☆

TESA GONZÁLEZ ● ▢
FLORISTELA

KEITA TAKAHASHI ● ▫
CHIKYUO

NUMI MIDORI ●
UNTITLED

JOANNA ZHOU ✤
HARAJUKU MOMIJI DOLLS

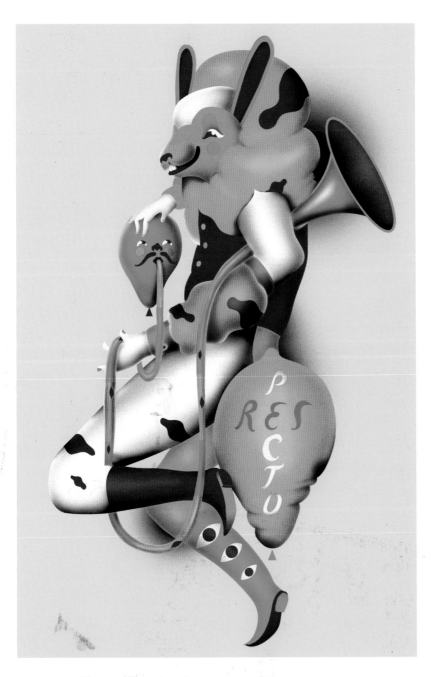

VILLE SAVIMAA ▢
RESPECTO

MIZNA WADA ✤
LOLLIPOP GIRL

● □ ▲ ♣ ☆

HELENA GARCIA □
TASMANIAN DEVIL

HELENA GARCIA ❑
BIRDWALK

ALICIA VARELA ⬤ ❑
LA VIDA REAL

● □ ▲ ♣ ☆

AGUSTÍN VIGUERA □
LUZ

GÉRALDINE COSNEAU □
MARIONNETTES

PASCAL VALDES ● □
GARAGE CLUB: THE BACKING SINGER

CLÉMENCE KERTUDO ● ▫
VIAJAR LIGERO

LA PRINCESITA ● ▫
DOMESTIC ANIMAL II

GENEVIÈVE GAUCKLER ☐
STRAWBERRY GIRL

DANIEL DÍAZ PIÑEIRO 🗆
DR.

DANIEL DÍAZ PIÑEIRO 🗆
PRIEST

AGU MÉNDEZ ● 🗆
FRIGO PIE CADUCAO'

●□▲♣☆

THINKD □
THE GUITARIST

ん
ふ
っ

AYAKO OKUBO & NHK ☐
TENSAI TV KUN - MONJI AND IRICA

NUMI MIDORI ●
CLARABELLA

●□▲♣☆

NAOSHI ●
PET DAUGHTER

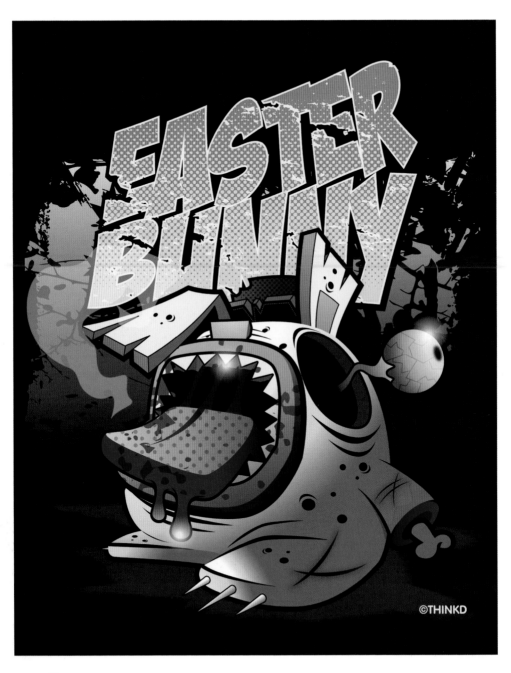

THINKD
EASTER BUNNY ZOMBIE

● □ ▲ ♣ ☆

FRAN FERRIZ □ ☆
ZOMBIES

OSCAR CHÁVEZ ❑
NIÑO ÁRBOL

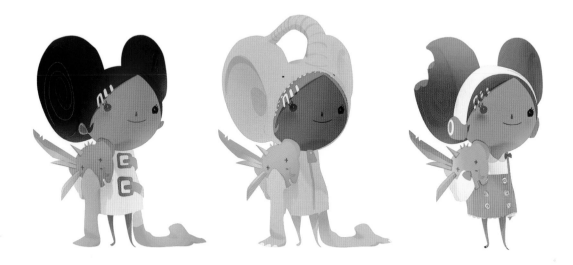

PERRY DIXON MAPLE
ELLIE

OSCAR CHÁVEZ
POLLO

ANNA FONT ●
SIN TÍTULO

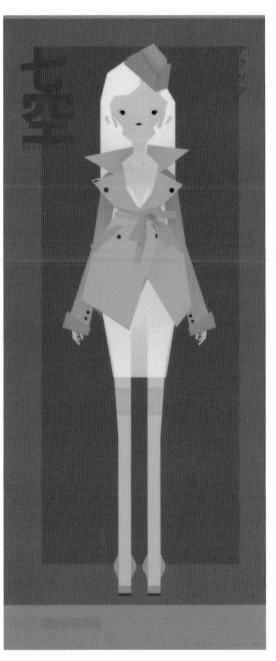

PERRY DIXON MAPLE ☐
ROSA

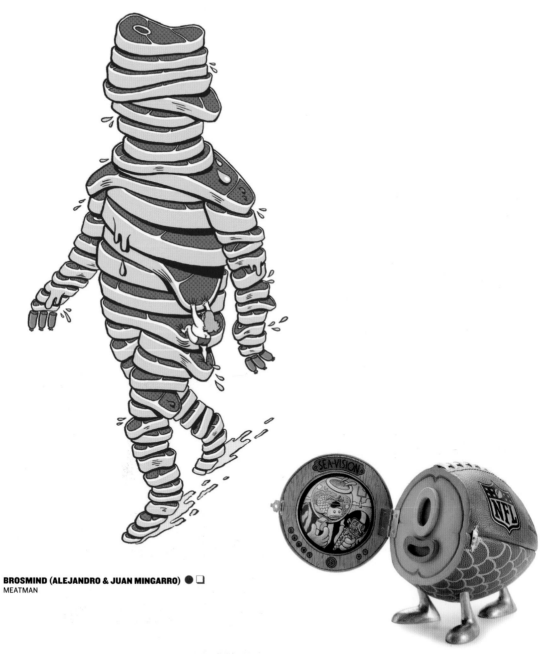

BROSMIND (ALEJANDRO & JUAN MINGARRO) ●□
MEATMAN

BROSMIND (ALEJANDRO & JUAN MINGARRO) ▲
NORMAN

RYAN CHAPMAN
CHOPPED

HEDOF ●□
RED BULL

RED NOSE STUDIO ● ☆
CLUTCH

MICHELA AIMI
LE BEIDES

YUBIA
BULLIT

YUBIA
BULLIT

RED NOSE STUDIO ● ☆
THE SEEDER

TESA GONZÁLEZ ●◻
GOSS

TESA GONZÁLEZ ●◻
MERLIMBERTO Y PATINETE

TESA GONZÁLEZ ●◻
REY GRANDE

SOYOUZGRAPHIC ☐
Z TEAM

GHOSTPATROL ●
POWER IN MUSHROOMS

TAKASHI HINODA ▲
THE WORLD

TAKASHI HINODA ▲
DEPRIVATION OF THE THRONE

GREG. "LEON" GUILLEMIN ❏
PAPER HEROES: PULP FICTION

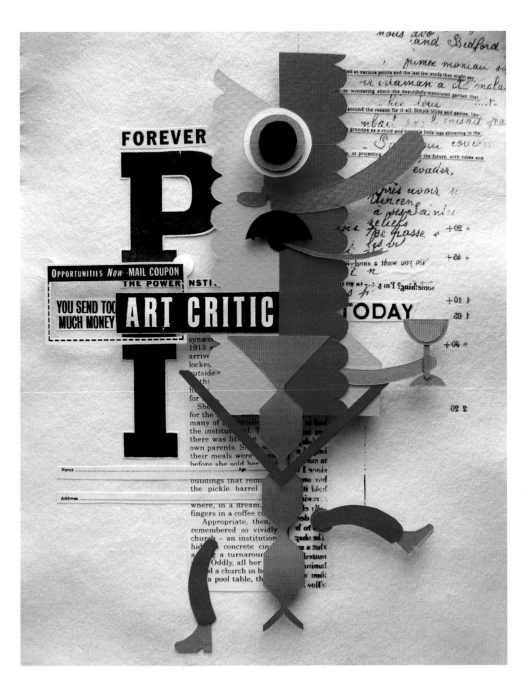

NICOLÁS NAZARENO SARSOTTI ●
FORMAS TEXTUALES

SONIA ESPLUGAS ● □
CACTOTEM 2

ORNE CABRITA ●
GUAPARO BIRD

OSCAR CHÁVEZ □
PASCUERO MALDITO

●□▲♣☆

MIZNA WADA □
AKAZUKIN

RORY MITCHELL □
FUNWAR CHARACTERS

THINKD
FIGHTO

● □ ▲ ♣ ☆

TANAKA SHIN ♣
BR.

AIIKO VOLSY ● □
HI!! JE SUIS UN MONSTRE!

GREG. "LEON" GUILLEMIN □
PAPER HEROES: HIT GIRL

WANSAIDE ☐
UNTITLED 2

MARK GMEHLING ☆
DRINSCH CHARACTER SERIES

GRELIN MACHIN ☆
BOB VAN CAROTID

JOÃO LAURO FONTE & JOHN PAUL ☐
IMAGINARY FRIEND

●□▲♣☆

DAN MATUTINA ♣
BOY & THE BIG BAD WOLF

PERRY DIXON MAPLE □
SOMBER AVELIN

ORNE CABRITA ●
ALIENAT

●□▲♣☆

TUOMAS IKONEN ♣
PAPER TOTEM !

SOYOUZGRAPHIC □
MODS VS ROCK

FRAN FERRIZ ☆ ☐
ROBOGIRL

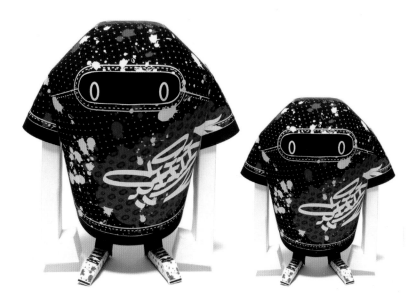

GILLES FRELUCHE ❑
STRIPTEASE

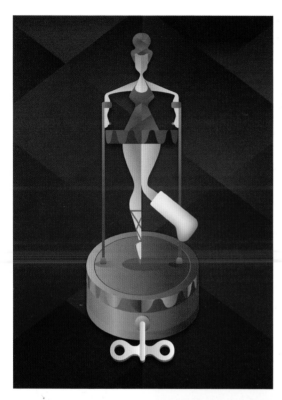

GILLES FRELUCHE ☐
BAILA CON DIOS

FRAN FERRIZ ☐ ☆
ALIEN TEAM

● □ ▲ ♣ ☆

GRELIN MACHIN □
HAPPY HALLOWEEN

DAN MATUTINA
AMATEURS

GRELIN MACHIN ❑
GLUTTONY

"FML"

HELENA GARCIA
FML

● □ ▲ ♣ ☆

ZOSEN □
LOVE WALKERS

AGENTE MORILLAS □
ONLY IN BRUSSELS

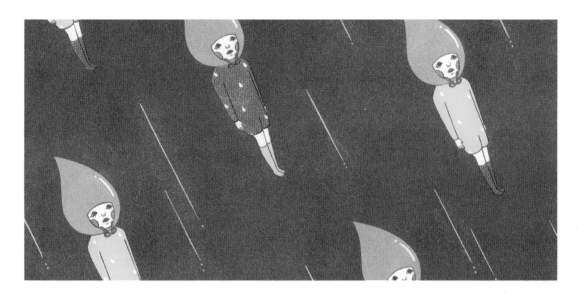

NAOSHI ●
RAIN BOYS - LET'S GO HOME NOW

DIANE KOSS ✤
CUTESY MONSTER MASCOT

ARNAUD BOUTIN ● ▢
MON PREMIER JOUR DE CLASSE

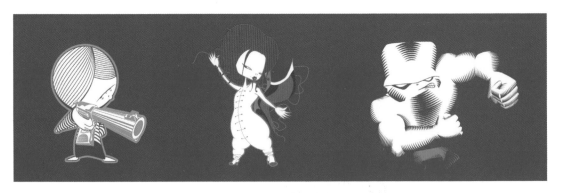

SOYOUZGRAPHIC ▢
SABLE BRUN

●□▲♣☆

GENEVIÈVE GAUCKLER □
PARIS

AGUSTÍN VIGUERA ☐
YARMIS

●□▲♣☆

AGENTE MORILLAS ❑
EL CORTADOR DE CÉSPED

RORY MITCHELL ❑
PREGNANT LADY

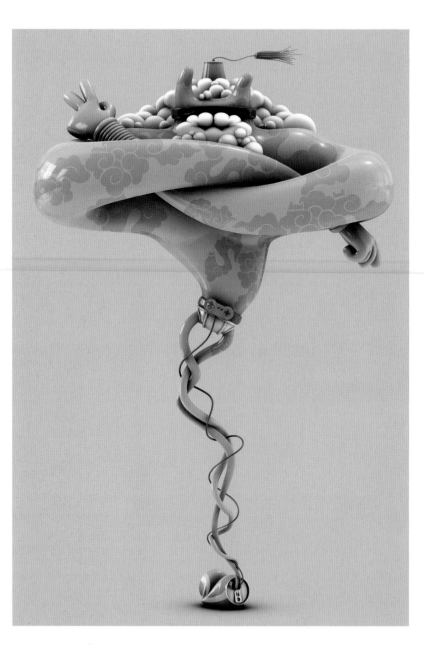

MARK GMEHLING ☆
DRINSCH CHARACTER SERIES

DIANE KOSS ✤
#I - FROM "HOME IS WHERE..." SERIES

EGGPICNIC ● ▢
(CAMILA DE GREGORIO,
CHRISTOPHER MACALUSO)
ONE OF THOSE DAYS

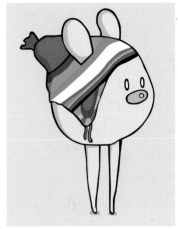

EGGPICNIC ● ▢
(CAMILA DE GREGORIO,
CHRISTOPHER MACALUSO)
ALTIPLÁNICO

TOY2R ✤
ROLITOBOY

TATALAB ▢
BURGUER BOY / DONUT BOY

DIANE KOSS ✤
THE AMERICAN DREAM - I AM NOT YOUR TOY

YUSAKU MAEDA ●
HUMANHUNTING

ZEPTONN □
KING OF THE DOTS

●□▲♣☆

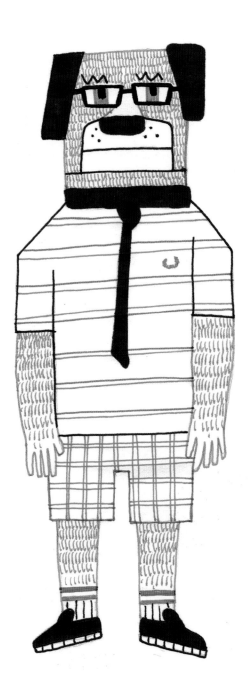

GUILLAUME PAIN – TOUGUI ✤
CROOKS GANG

RORY MITCHELL ☐
KNIGHT

SERGIO MORA ●□
LUVE SONGS

● □ ▲ ♣ ☆

SERGIO MORA ● □
MAGRITTE CANIBAL

YUBIA ●▢
MATRIUSKA

● □ ▲ ♣ ☆

CLÉMENCE KERTUDO ● □
HIBU TIPOGRÁFICO

AGU MÉNDEZ
PEQUEÑOS DICTADORES

●□▲♣☆

ANNA FONT ●
SIN TÍTULO

TAKASHI HINODA ▲
ZOMBIE BROTHERS

SOYOUZGRAPHIC ☐
B.Z.T.

● □ ▲ ♣ ☆

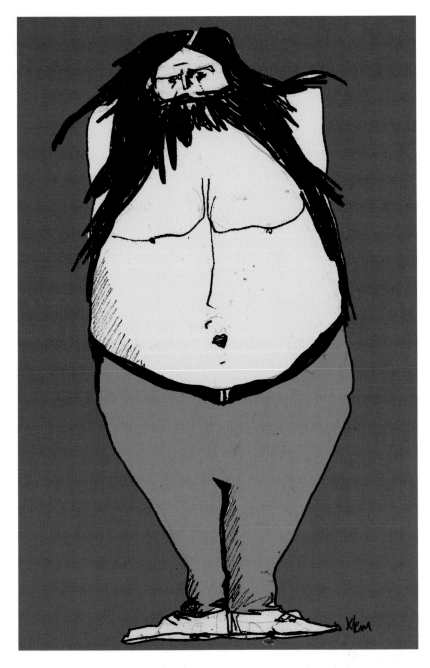

CLÉMENCE KERTUDO ● □
HOMBRE MUJER

TECHNO IMAGE - TIAGO HOISEL
THIS HAS NEVER HAPPENED TO ME BEFORE...

● ◻ ▲ ♣ ☆

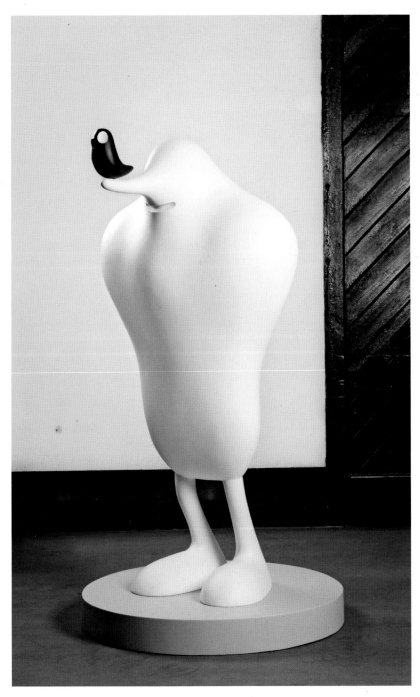

BROSMIND ▲
(ALEJANDRO & JUAN MINGARRO)
LARRY

TUOMAS IKONEN ● ▢
PAMPER YOUR BRAIN

MARTIN HSU ●
SEA MONKEE FERRY

OSCAR CHÁVEZ ❑
9 DE TRÉBOL

AGU MÉNDEZ ● ☐
WHO'S JACOB

JEAN JULLIEN ●
THE REPUBLIC

AGENTE MORILLAS ❏
SIN TÍTULO

FRANK PLANT ▲
FOREST FOR THE TREES

GINA THORSTENSEN ✤
STØVDOTT

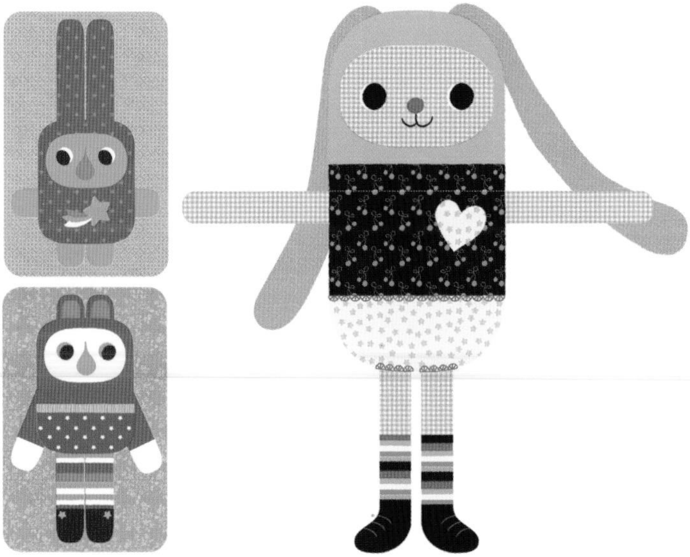

GÉRALDINE COSNEAU
MINI-HÉROS

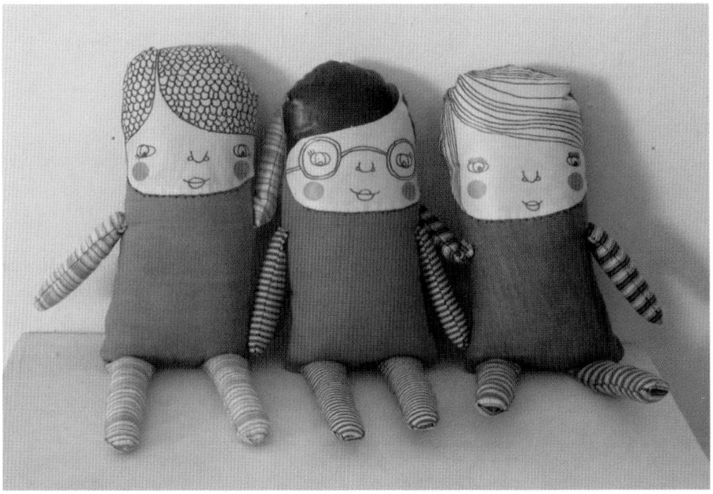

ANNA FONT
MUÑECAS

JIM WHITTAMORE
KENZIE

EGGPICNIC (CAMILA DE GREGORIO, CHRISTOPHER MACALUSO) ✣
TIRANITO, LA VIDA ES UNA FIESTA

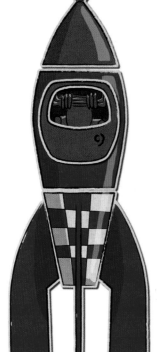

ANDRÉS RODRÍGUEZ ☐
DR. W.

GUILLAUME PAIN – TOUGUI ✣
LUMBER JACK

RED NOSE STUDIO ● ☆
FOUR ARM

RUMPUS ANIMATION ▢
RUMPUS NEW YORK

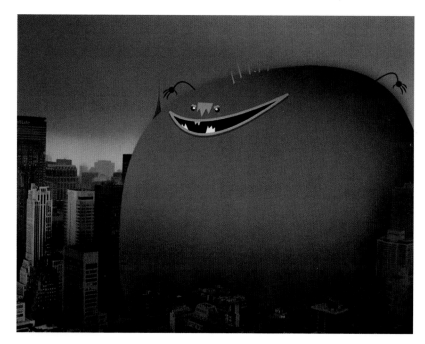

RED NOSE STUDIO ● ☆
STILTY

STÉPHANE MUNNIER ❑
TULULU

TOY2R ✢
3.5" BABY QEE - LUNNA EDITION

FRAN FERRIZ ☐☆
ALIEN ENCOUNTER

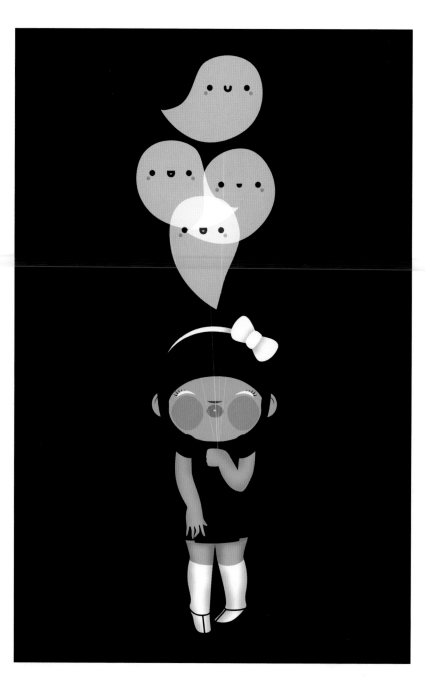

LA PRINCESITA ☐
MUERTITA

● ▢ ▲ ♣ ☆

TECHNO IMAGE
TIAGO HOISEL & PEDRO CONTI ☆
LADYBUG

TECHNO IMAGE - TIAGO HOISEL ▢
DALÍ

●□▲♣☆

THUNDERCUT ●
FRIDGE FRIENDS

ARIAN [ZAL] NOVEIR ☐
SUPER HEROES: PAINTED – HULK

●□▲♣☆

THINKD □
BUNNY CRY

MUTTO – GUILLE MUÑOZ ❑
HUNDMANN

GENEVIÈVE GAUCKLER ❑
TIED UP

●□▲♣☆

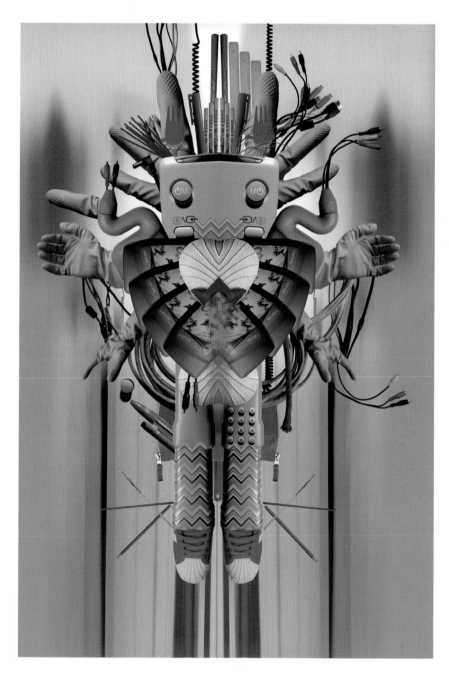

GENEVIÈVE GAUCKLER □
MANDALA #10

PEZ ●
CORREQUETEPILLO

●□▲♣☆

MALICIA ●
RICH BITCH

MALICIA ●
VENENO

YUSAKU MAEDA ●▢
ZOMBIE

MIKEL CASAL ● ▢
ECOSISTEMA

● □ ▲ ♣ ☆

御入学御祝

奇的高校

AYAKO OKUBO □
KITEKI HIGH SCHOOL

GINA THORSTENSEN ❖
GUSTAVO

●□▲♣☆

GINA THORSTENSEN ♣
CAMILLA

RORY MITCHELL ☐
ROCKETMAN

● □ ▲ ♣ ☆

TANAKA SHIN ♣
THREE

JEAN JULLIEN ● □
FAMILY

MICRO.BARBI ▲
BODOQUES

JOANNA ZHOU ●□
HARAJUKU ARMY

THUNDERCUT ●
HELLO NASSAU

PASCAL VALDES ●▢
GARAGE CLUB: THE NEIGHBOURS

ZEPTONN ▢
SQUIDOO BADGES

AYAKO OKUBO & TSUKASA YUNOUE
COMMANDERS IN THE LAST EAST

● □ ▲ ✤ ☆

TANAKA SHIN ✤
HOOPHY

RILLA ALEXANDER ✤
IDEA TOYS

TOY2R ✤
2.5" 1000TH QEE - CLEAR BOXEE HEAD

●□▲♣☆

GENEVIÈVE GAUCKLER ☐
FUTURE

ZOSEN
HÁBITOS ALIMENTICIOS

TOY2R ✤
A MIXED SHOT OF 2.5" QEES

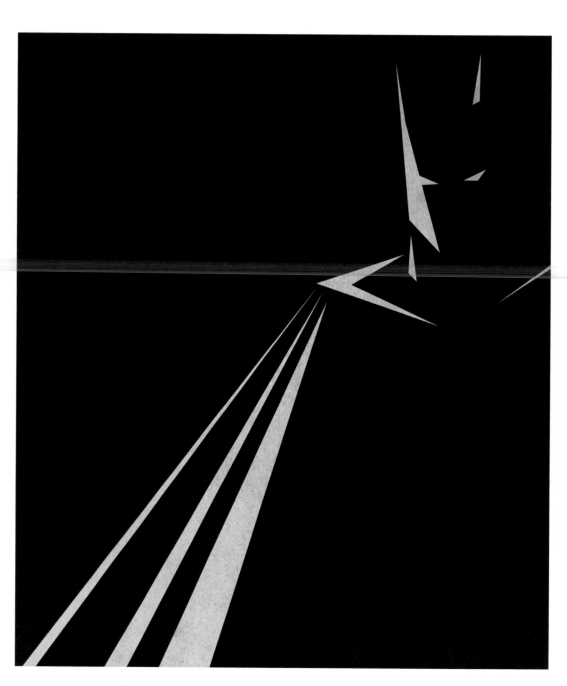

GREG. "LEON" GUILLEMIN ❏
PAPER HEROES: BATMAN DARK

WANSAIDE ❏
UNTITLED 3

TOY2R ♣
KID 666 FIGURE (NADA ONE)

SANTIAGO DURIEUX ❏
RUNNING DAY

HAPPYMIAOW ☆
MONSTER ALBUM

RYAN CHAPMAN ●❑
ONE MAN BAND

JOAQUÍN ALDEGUER ●❑
MONSTRUITO

FEDERICO ORRÙ ❑
ALAN MCSCARPE

FEDERICO ORRÙ ❑
OSVALDO HA FATTO AMICIZIA

AGENTE MORILLAS
EL RESPLANDOR

MIZNA WADA ❑
ZIGOKKU ENMA

JAVI MEDIALDEA ❑
GODZILLA

JAVI MEDIALDEA ❑
RIKISHI

HARUKA SHINJI ●☐
BATPHONIST

ANDRÉS RODRÍGUEZ ☐
LA EVOLUCIÓN - DR. W.

SEBASTIÁN BANDIN ●
THINK

GUY BLOOM ❑
BANJO

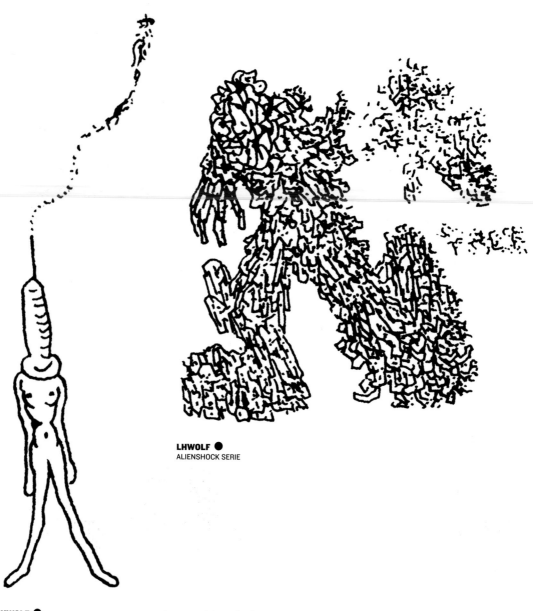

LHWOLF ●
ALIENSHOCK SERIE

LHWOLF ●
ALIENSHOCK SERIE

PARQUERAMA STUDIOS ●
ANGEL IN HAIRDRESSER

LHWOLF ●
ALIENSHOCK SERIE

PARQUERAMA STUDIOS ●
CONFETTI

CHARACTER DESIGN PROCESSES

PROCESSUS DE DESIGN DES PERSONNAGES

PROCESOS EN EL DISEÑO DE PERSONAJES

PROCESSI NEL DISEGNO DI PERSONAGGI

PENDIENTE
GUADALUPE LABAKÉ & NICOLÁS SÁNCHEZ

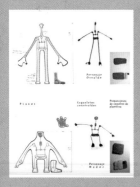

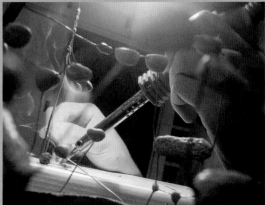

The design of these figures allows their shoulders to be manoeuvred independently. The tips of their feet are weighted to the ground using screws, around which a single copper wire is wound and soldered. They are then covered with putty and coated with plasticine mixed with hair wax, increasing their elasticity and preventing them cracking.

La conception de ces figurines permet à leurs épaules d'être articulées indépendamment. La pointe de leurs pieds est fixée au sol avec des vis, autour desquelles un fil de cuivre est enroulé et soudé. Ils sont ensuite recouverts de mastic et enduits de pâte à modeler mélangée avec du gel à cheveux pour augmenter leur élasticité et empêcher les fissures.

El diseño de estas figuras permite que sus hombros puedan ser manipulados de forma independiente. Las puntas de los pies se sujetan al suelo con tornillos, alrededor de los cuales se enrolla y suelda un alambre de cobre. Después se cubren con masilla y se revisten con plastilina mezclada con cera de pelo para aumentar su elasticidad y evitar que se agrieten.

Il disegno di queste figure permette di muovere le spalle in modo indipendente. Le punte dei piedi sono fissate al suolo con viti attorno alle quali è avvolto e saldato un singolo filo di rame. Le figure sono poi completate con stucco e ricoperte di plastilina mescolata a cera per capelli, così da aumentare la loro elasticità e impedire la formazione di crepe.

MANTIS
PERRY DIXON MAPLE

This character was rendered digitally follow-ing initial drawings in pencil and highlighter. The artist favoured shapes over lines in the design process, with colour playing a vital role. The visual inspiration was the clichéd "bombshell" sexy member of a game line-up, in particular the characters of the artist's childhood and the images and personalities they evoked.

Initialement dessiné au crayon et surligneur ce personnage est ensuite restitué numéri-quement. L'artiste a privilégié les formes aux lignes, les couleurs jouant ici un rôle primor-dial. L'inspiration vient du cliché de la joueuse pulpeuse et super canon, membre d'une équipe sportive, en particulier des person-nages de son enfance et des images et personnalités qu'elles lui évoquent.

Este personaje se digitalizó a partir de unos dibujos iniciales a lápiz y rotulador. El artista destacó más las formas que las líneas en el proceso de diseño, en el que el color desempeña un papel vital. Se inspiró visualmente en la estereotipada chica explosiva y sexy del elenco de un juego, en particular, los personajes de su infancia y las imágenes y personalidades que evocaban.

Questo personaggio è stato digitalizzato a partire dai disegni iniziali a matita e pennarello. Nel processo, l'artista ha dato la preferenza alle forme rispetto alle linee, con i colori che giocano un ruolo fondamentale. L'ispirazione visiva proviene dallo stereotipato personaggio tipo "bomba sexy" dei giochi, in particolare dai caratteri della sua gioventù e dalle immagini e personalità evocate.

RUPERTO
PAULA CELINA RAMOS

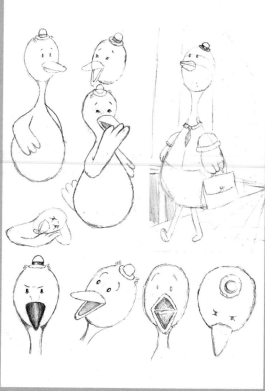

Rendered in India ink on illustration paper, this sweet little story follows Ruperto, a bird-cum-office-worker who cheers up his new friend by taking her for a ride. The illustrator accentuated the humour of the character by basing its design on lopsided birds like flamingos, with long, thin necks and heads much smaller than their bodies.

Réalisée à l'encre de chine cette adorable histoire suit Ruperto, un oiseau employé de bureau qui distrait sa nouvelle amie en l'emmenant faire un tour. L'illustratrice accentue l'humour du personnage en s'inspirant d'oiseaux mal proportionnés, comme les flamants, avec des cous longs et fins et des têtes bien plus petites que leurs corps.

Dibujada en tinta china sobre papel ilustración, esta pequeña y dulce historia sigue a Ruperto, un pájaro oficinista que anima a su nueva amiga llevándola de paseo. La ilustradora acentuó los rasgos humorísticos del personaje basando su diseño en las aves desproporcionadas, como los flamencos, de cuellos largos y delgados y cabezas mucho más pequeñas que sus cuerpos.

Resa in inchiostro di china su carta da illustrazione, questa breve e tenera storia segue Ruperto, un uccello trasformato in impiegato che tira su il morale della sua nuova amica portandola a fare un giro. L'illustratore ha accentuato la natura umoristica del personaggio basando il disegno su uccelli "sproporzionati", del tipo dei fenicotteri, con il collo lungo e sottile e la testa molto più piccola del corpo.

THE MECHANIC
ASHER B. EGGLESTON

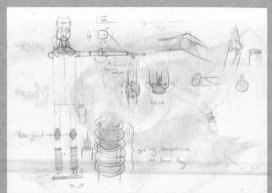

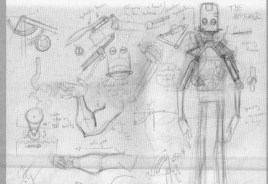

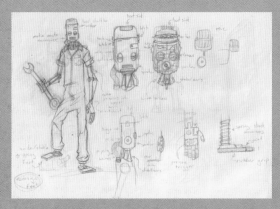

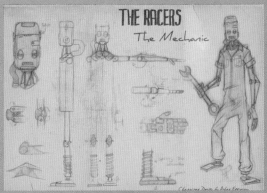

Designed using Prismacolor Col-Erase coloured pencil on smooth drawing paper, the story of The Mechanic revolves around three main figures from a hover bike racing team (a robotic Mechanic, Otto and Jane). The feel and style of the story is inspired by 1920s machinery and early board-track motorcycle racing.

Dessiné avec des crayons de couleurs Prismacolor Col-Erase sur du papier dessin lisse, The Mechanic s'articule autour de trois personnages principaux d'une équipe de course de *hoverbike* (un mécanicien robotisé, Otto et Jane). L'atmosphère et le style de l'histoire sont inspirés des machines des années 20 et des premiers circuits de course motos.

3D Model by Jay Miller

Diseñada con lápiz de color Prismacolor Col-Erase sobre papel de dibujo liso, la historia de The Mechanic gira en torno a tres figuras principales de un equipo de carreras de motos voladoras (un mecánico robotizado, Otto y Jane). El aspecto y el estilo de la historia se inspiran en la maquinaria de la década de los 1920 y en las primeras carreras de motociclismo en autódromos.

Disegnata con matita colorata Prismacolor Col-Erase su carta da disegno liscia, la storia di The Mechanic gira attorno a tre personaggi principali che gareggiano su motociclette volanti (un meccanico robotizzato, Otto e Jane). Lo stile e l'atmosfera della storia sono ispirati ai macchinari degli anni 1920 e alle prime gare di motociclismo in pista.

ROBOT
FRANCISCO ALBERT ALBUSAC

After defining the figure through copious sketching, the artist proceeds to consider the setting, light and colours. Background elements like the sky and ground help solidify the palette. Realism is ensured through subtle touches, such as the dash of violet at the top and the use of complementary colours to offset the dominant tones and shadows.

Après avoir défini la forme grâce à une quantité abondante d'esquisses, l'artiste passe au décor, à la lumière et aux couleurs. Les éléments d'arrière plan comme le ciel et la terre permettent de renforcer la palette. Le réalisme est apporté par touches subtiles, comme un soupçon de violet et par l'utilisation de couleurs complémentaires pour contrebalancer les ombres et les tons dominants.

Tras definir la figura después de numerosos bocetos, el artista procede a considerar la composición, la luz y los colores. Los elementos del fondo, como el cielo y la tierra, ayudan a solidificar la paleta. El realismo se consigue mediante pinceladas sutiles, como el toque violeta en la parte superior y el uso de colores complementarios para compensar los tonos y sombras dominantes.

Dopo una copiosa fase di sketching per definire la figura, l'artista è passato a considerare lo scenario, la luce e i colori, dove gli elementi di sfondo come il cielo e il terreno aiutano a consolidare la paletta. Il realismo è assicurato da tocchi quasi impercettibili, come le tracce di violetto in testa e l'uso di colori complementari per compensare toni dominanti e ombre.

ALLÁ VA EL ROBOT
JOAQUÍN ALDEGUER

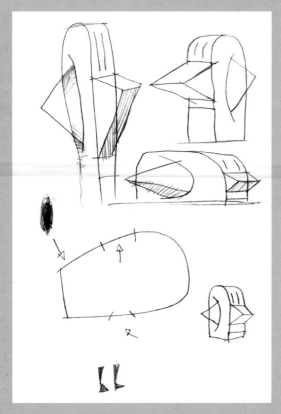

Initially sketched and then digitised, this anonymous robot and its companion are inspired by the primitive robots of 1950s film. It is deliberately dishevelled and un-kempt, in keeping with this series' underlying humour. An amorphous blob flanked by a head and legs, attached to its body is a swirly spiral of fuzz, which follows it wherever it goes.

D'abord dessiné puis numérisé, ce robot anonyme et son compagnon sont inspirés des robots primitifs du cinéma des années 50. Intentionnellement brouillon et négligé le style correspond à l'humour sous-jacent de cette série. Boule informe flanquée d'une tête et de deux jambes, une touffe de poils en spirale, attachée à son corps, le suit partout où il va.

Este robot anónimo y su compañero, esboza-dos primero y posteriormente digitalizados, están inspirados en los robots primitivos de los filmes de los cincuenta. Su aspecto es deliberadamente desaliñado y descuidado, en consonancia con el humor que recorre la serie: un pegote amorfo flanqueado por una cabeza y unas piernas, con una espiral de pelusa pegada a su cuerpo que le sigue allá donde va.

Schizzato prima e digitalizzato poi, questo robot anonimo e il suo compagno sono ispirati ai robot primitivi dei film degli anni 1950, deliberatamente sciatti e trasandati in armo-nia con lo humour sottinteso nella serie. Un ovoide amorfo provvisto di testa e gambe, sul cui corpo è attaccata una spirale di peluria arrotolata che lo segue ovunque.

CURLING PLAYERS
FABRICE LE NEZET

Designed and printed in 3D, the final copies of this series were rendered in thermoplastic polyurethane using silicone moulds. The project presented the challenge of making a sport widely considered boring seem modern and fresh. Blending elegance, humanity and modernity, the shapes are simultaneously minimalist, urban, rough, messy and fun. They combine toy-like properties with sculpture.

Conçues et imprimées en 3D, les reproductions définitives de cette série sont réalisées en polyuréthane thermoplastique dans des moules en silicone. Le projet présente un sport communément jugé ennuyeux comme moderne et frais. Mélange d'élégance, d'humanité et de modernité, les formes sont à la fois minimalistes, urbaines, brutes, négligées et amusantes. Une alliance des caractéristiques du *toy* et de la sculpture.

Diseñadas e impresas en 3D, las copias finales de la serie se hicieron en poliuretano termoplástico usando moldes de silicona. El proyecto presentaba el desafío de hacer que un deporte comúnmente considerado aburrido parezca moderno y fresco. Con una mezcla de elegancia, humanidad y modernidad, las formas son a la vez minimalistas, urbanas, duras, descuidadas y divertidas. Combinan características propias de los *toys* con la escultura.

Disegnate e stampate in 3D, le copie finali di questa serie sono state rese in poliuretano termoplastico con stampi in silicone. Il progetto presentava la sfida di trasformare uno sport comunemente ritenuto noioso in un'attività fresca moderna. Riunendo eleganza, umanità e modernità, le forme sono allo stesso tempo minimaliste, urbane, toste, trasandate e simpatiche, combinando proprietà di *toy* con attributi di scultura.

ARTIST INTERVIEWS

ENTRETIENS AVEC DES ARTISTES

ENTREVISTAS A ARTISTAS

INTERVISTE CON ARTISTI

FERNANDO FALCO-NE

Fernando Falcone was born in 1977 in Buenos Aires, Argentina, where he currently lives. He trained at the Prilidiano Pueyrredón National School of Fine Arts from 1997-2002, and in 2006 began illustrating for major publishers and advertising agencies in countries such as Argentina, Spain, Nicaragua, the Netherlands, Brazil, France and China. He uses a wide range of techniques in his work, including pencil, oils, watercolours and tempera, often fusing these materials in various combinations and editing them digitally.

Fernando Falcone est né en 1977 à Buenos Aires, en Argentine, où il vit aujourd'hui. Il a fait ses études à l'École nationale supérieure des beaux-arts Prilidiano Pueyrrédon de 1997 à 2002. En 2006, il commence à travailler en tant qu'illustrateur pour d'importants éditeurs et agences de publicités dans des pays comme l'Argentine, l'Espagne, le Nicaragua, les Pays-Bas, le Brésil, la France, et la Chine. Il utilise un large panel de techniques dans son travail, comme le crayon, la peinture à l'huile, l'aquarelle, la tempéra, et mélange ces matériaux en diverses combinaisons et les édite numériquement.

HOW WOULD YOU DEFINE YOUR PERSONAL STYLE?

I'm not too sure: I think that visual art defines itself in each image we create. I'm interested in conveying ambiguity through my characters. I subscribe to the idea that the dark often contains more beauty than the light. There is an unconscious tendency to see white as good and black as bad. I disagree with this notion, and seek to interrogate it in my work.

HOW DID YOU COME TO WORK IN THE WORLD OF ILLUSTRATION?

I think illustrating and painting can be quite similar, but they differ in the way work is published. The intimacy in our relationship with books was something I always found interesting and which influenced my decision to go down this route. I found it easy to adapt to illustrating literary pieces because my work has always been somewhat narrative.

COMMENT DÉFINIRIEZ-VOUS VOTRE STYLE ?

Je ne sais pas trop : je pense que l'art graphique se définit par lui-même dans chaque image que nous créons. Je cherche à transmettre l'ambiguïté de mes personnages. Je partage l'idée que l'obscur a bien plus de beauté que la lumière. Il existe une tendance à percevoir ce qui est blanc comme bon et mauvais ce qui est noir. Je ne suis pas d'accord avec cette idée et je la remets en cause dans mon travail.

COMMENT EN ÊTES-VOUS ARRIVÉ À TRAVAILLER DANS LE MONDE DE L'ILLUSTRATION ?

Je pense que l'illustration et la peinture ont des points communs mais la façon dont le travail est publié diffère. Notre rapport intime au livre m'a toujours intéressé et motivé à poursuivre dans cette voie. Je trouve facile de m'adapter aux

Fernando Falcone nació en 1977 en Buenos Aires, Argentina, donde vive actualmente. Estudió en la Escuela Nacional de Bellas Artes Prilidiano Pueyrredón entre los años 1997 y 2002. A partir del año 2006 empezó a colaborar como ilustrador en importantes editoriales de Argentina, España, Francia, Nicaragua y China, así como en diferentes agencias de publicidad de Argentina, Brasil, Francia, España y Holanda. Las técnicas que utiliza son variadas y abarcan desde el dibujo con lápices, óleo, acuarelas y témperas a distintas combinaciones de dichos materiales con retoque digital.

Fernando Falcone è nato nel 1977 a Buenos Aires, Argentina, dove risiede attualmente. Dal 1997 al 2002 ha studiato alla Scuola Nazionale di Belle Arti Prilidiano Pueyrredón, poi a partire dal 2006 ha iniziato a collaborare come illustratore per importanti case editrici in Argentina, Spagna, Francia, Nicaragua e Cina, oltre a diverse agenzie pubblicitarie in Argentina, Brasile, Francia, Spagna e Olanda. Utilizza svariate tecniche, dal disegno a pastello, olio, acquarello e tempera a diverse combinazioni di questi materiali con ritocchi digitali.

¿CÓMO DEFINIRÍAS TU ESTILO?

No estoy muy seguro, pienso que el arte visual se autodefine en cada imagen que creamos. Me interesa transmitir ambigüedad en los personajes. Me identifico con la idea de que lo oscuro muchas veces puede contener más belleza que lo luminoso. Inconscientemente se piensa que lo blanco es bueno y lo negro es malo. No estoy de acuerdo con esas ideas y me interesa plantearlo en mis trabajos.

¿QUÉ TE LLEVÓ A DEDICARTE AL MUNDO DE LA ILUSTRACIÓN?

Creo que hacer ilustraciones y pintar cuadros puede ser bastante parecido, pero la manera de publicar es diferente. Existe cierta intimidad en la relación que tenemos con un libro; eso siempre me resultó interesante y determinó mi decisión de seguir este camino. Me adapté bien a ilustrar obras literarias porque siempre tuve un estilo narrativo en mis trabajos.

COME DEFINIRESTI IL TUO STILE PERSONALE?

Non sarei molto sicuro. Credo che l'arte visiva si autodefinisca in ogni immagine che creiamo. Mi interessa trasmettere ambiguità nei personaggi e mi identifico con l'idea che molte volte ciò che è oscuro può contenere più bellezza di ciò che è luminoso. Inconsciamente associamo il bianco con il buono e il nero con il cattivo. Non sono d'accordo con queste idee e cerco di metterle in discussione nelle mie opere.

CHE COSA TI HA PORTATO A OPERARE NEL MONDO DELL'ILLUSTRAZIONE?

Credo che dedicarsi alle illustrazioni e dipingere quadri possano essere abbastanza simili, anche se il modo di pubblicare è diverso. Nella nostra relazione con un libro esiste una certa intimità, aspetto che ho sempre trovato interessante e che ha influito nella mia decisione di prendere questa strada. Mi sono adattato a illustrare opere letterarie

**WHAT DIFFERENCES AND SIMILARI-
TIES ARE THERE BETWEEN WHAT YOU
DRAW TODAY AND WHAT YOU USED TO
DRAW AS A CHILD?**
Beyond technical differences, there aren't
too many. Though I always try to keep
seeing drawing and painting through the
same eyes I did when I was a child, it can
be hard to keep up this playful spirit when
you've got tight deadlines to meet. You
have to take your work a lot less seriously
than you might think if you want to keep
your creativity intact.

**WHAT GOES THROUGH YOUR MIND
WHEN YOU ARE CREATING A NEW
CHARACTER?**
If the character is based on a text, I read
the story and descriptions and then make
lots of sketches. I like to play around with
proportion and lack of proportion. It's a
long process and I'm not satisfied until
I find the charm in the character. I am
always mindful that I'm going to have
to draw the character on more than one
occasion and in different contexts. I have
to ensure this repetition doesn't bore
or tire me.

DESCRIBE YOUR IDEAL PROJECT.
It would involve writing and illustrating
a book in which I can develop ideas and
characters with total narrative and aes-
thetic freedom, without being conditioned
by another person's text or by an editor.

illustrations d'œuvres littéraires parce
que mon travail a toujours été proche
de celui de la narration.

**QUELLES SONT LES DIFFÉRENCES
ET LES SIMILARITÉS ENTRE VOTRE
MANIÈRE DE DESSINER AUJOURD'HUI
ET DURANT VOTRE ENFANCE ?**
Au delà des différences techniques, il n'y
en a pas tant que ça. Bien que j'essaie toujours de voir les peintures et les dessins
avec les yeux de l'enfance, c'est parfois
difficile de conserver cet esprit ludique
quand on doit respecter des délais très
serrés. On doit prendre son travail bien
moins au sérieux qu'on pourrait le penser
si on veut garder sa créativité intacte.

**A QUOI PENSEZ-VOUS QUAND VOUS
CRÉEZ UN NOUVEAU PERSONNAGE ?**
Si le personnage est issu d'un texte, je lis
l'histoire et les descriptions et ensuite je
fais beaucoup d'esquisses. J'aime m'amu-
ser avec les proportions et l'absence de
proportion. C'est un long processus et je
ne suis satisfait qu'après avoir trouvé du
charme au personnage. J'ai toujours à
l'esprit que je vais devoir dessiner ce personnage plus d'une fois et dans différents
contextes. Je dois m'assurer que cette
répétition ne m'ennuie et ne me fatigue pas.

DÉCRIVEZ VOTRE PROJET IDÉAL.
Ce un projet qui me permettrait d'écrire
et d'illustrer un livre dans lequel je peux
développer des idées et des personnages
avec une liberté de narration et d'esthétique, sans être influencé par le texte
d'une autre personne ou par un éditeur.

¿CUÁLES SON LAS DIFERENCIAS Y LAS SIMILITUDES ENTRE LO QUE DIBUJAS HOY EN DÍA Y LO QUE DIBUJABAS CUANDO ERAS PEQUEÑO?

No hay tantas diferencias, más allá de las técnicas. Aunque siempre intento ver el dibujo y la pintura como cuando era chico, es difícil mantener ese espíritu lúdico cuando estás apurado con plazos de entrega. Creo que para lograr que la creatividad se mantenga intacta hay que tomarse este trabajo con menos seriedad de lo que uno imaginaría.

¿QUÉ PASA POR TU CABEZA CUANDO ESTÁS CREANDO UN NUEVO PERSONAJE?

Si está inspirado en un texto, leo la historia, las descripciones y principalmente hago muchos bocetos. Juego con las proporciones y las desproporciones. Es un proceso largo, y no quedo conforme hasta que no encuentro alguna gracia en el personaje que estoy haciendo. Durante la creación de un personaje, siempre tengo en cuenta que voy a dibujarlo muchas veces y en diferentes situaciones. Tengo que lograr que no me aburra ni me canse esa repetición.

DESCRIBE TU PROYECTO IDEAL.

Escribir e ilustrar un libro donde pueda desarrollar ideas y personajes sin estar condicionado por un texto de otra persona, o por un editor. Trabajar con total libertad, tanto en la historia como en la estética.

perché nelle mie opere ho sempre avuto uno stile narrativo.

QUALI SONO LE DIFFERENZE E LE SIMILITUDINI TRA QUELLO CHE DISEGNI ORA E QUELLO CHE DISEGNAVI QUANDO ERI PICCOLO?

Al di là delle tecniche, non ci sono molte differenze. Anche se cerco sempre di vedere il disegno e la pittura come quando ero bambino, è difficile conservare quello spirito ludico quando sei assillato da scadenze di consegna. Credo che per riuscire a mantenere intatta la creatività sia necessario prendere questo lavoro con meno serietà di quanto ci si possa immaginare.

CHE COSA TI PASSA PER LA TESTA MENTRE CREI UN NUOVO PERSONAGGIO?

Se il personaggio è ispirato a un testo, leggo la storia, le descrizioni e soprattutto preparo molti bozzetti. Gioco con le proporzioni e le sproporzioni. È un processo lungo e non mi considero soddisfatto finché non trovo del fascino nel personaggio che sto costruendo. Durante la creazione di un personaggio tengo sempre presente che lo disegnerò molte volte e in diverse situazioni. Devo fare in modo che questa reiterazione non mi annoi né mi stanchi.

DESCRIVI IL TUO PROGETTO IDEALE.

Scrivere e illustrare un libro in cui sia possibile sviluppare idee e personaggi senza essere condizionato da testi di altre persone o da un editor. Lavorare con libertà totale, sia nella storia sia negli aspetti estetici.

NATHAN JUOGVICIUS

Nathan Jurevicius has worked as a freelance illustrator and artist for many international companies and publications. His most acclaimed project, Scarygirl, was created in 2001, and has since developed a worldwide underground following through its online comic, limited edition vinyl toys, designer products and exhibitions. Nathan released his first graphic novel, based on Scarygirl, with Australia's leading independent publisher, Allen & Unwin. Its various accolades include the 2009 Aurealis Award for Best Illustrated Book/Graphic Novel. In 2009 Nathan launched the Scarygirl online game in conjunction with Passion Pictures Australia. It has surpassed the 1 million player mark.

Nathan Jurevicius a travaillé comme illustrateur et artiste pour de nombreuses publications et compagnies internationales. Son projet le plus acclamé, Scarygirl, créé en 2001, continue de conquérir un large public *underground* dans le monde entier via sa bande dessinée en ligne, l'édition limitée de *vinyl toys*, des objets design et des expositions. Nathan a publié son premier roman graphique, basé sur Scarygirl, avec le leader des éditeurs indépendants australiens, Allen & Unwin. Le prix Aurealis 2009 du meilleur roman graphique figure parmi ses diverses récompenses. En 2009 Nathan lance, avec Passion Picture Australia, le jeu en ligne Scarygirl qui compte plus d'un million de joueurs.

HOW WOULD YOU DEFINE YOUR PERSONAL STYLE?

Narrative and character-driven, myth-inspired art with a strong focus on Lithuanian culture.

WHAT GOES THROUGH YOUR MIND WHEN YOU ARE CREATING A NEW CHARACTER?

Generally there's a lot of pre-planning on how the character fits into the universe I'm creating visually: what the possible back-story could be and how it interacts with other characters in that world.

HOW DID YOU GET YOUR FIRST MAJOR COMMISSION?

I was still at university and was asked by my lecturer if I would be interested in discussing a project with an alternative religious publisher. I ended up illustrating six children's books for them about a flying cloud that explores ancient stories.

COMMENT DÉFINIRIEZ-VOUS VOTRE STYLE PERSONNEL?

Mon style est axé sur le récit et les personnages, un art inspiré par la mythologie avec un fort accent sur la culture lituanienne.

QUE SE PASSE-T-IL DANS VOTRE ESPRIT LORSQUE VOUS CRÉEZ UN NOUVEAU PERSONNAGE?

En général il y a un long préparatif fait au préalable, à savoir comment le personnage s'intègre à l'univers esthétique que je crée, quel serait son parcours et sa relation aux autres personnages dans ce monde.

COMMENT AVEZ-VOUS OBTENU VOTRE PREMIÈRE COMMANDE IMPORTANTE ?

J'étais encore à l'université et mon professeur m'a demandé si cela m'intéressait de discuter d'un projet avec une maison d'édition religieuse alternative. J'ai fini

Nathan Jurevicius ha trabajado como ilustrador y artista *freelance* para muchas empresas y publicaciones internacionales. En 2001 creó Scarygirl, su proyecto más aclamado, y desde entonces ha desarrollado un *underground* internacional que ha culminado con un cómic en línea, juguetes de vinilo de edición limitada, artículos de diseño y exposiciones. Nathan publicó su primera novela gráfica, basada en Scarygirl, en la principal editorial independiente de Australia, Allen & Unwin. Entre sus distinciones figura el Premio Aurealis 2009 al Mejor Libro Ilustrado/Novela Gráfica. En 2009 Nathan lanzó el juego en línea Scarygirl junto con Passion Pictures Australia. Ya ha superado la marca del millón de jugadores.

Nathan Jurevicius ha operato come illustratore e artista freelance per diverse società e pubblicazioni internazionali. Il suo progetto più noto e apprezzato, Scarygirl, è stato creato nel 2001 e da allora ha sviluppato un *underground* a livello mondiale attraverso fumetti online, *toys* in vinile a edizione limitata, prodotti di design e mostre. Nathan ha realizzato il suo primo romanzo grafico, basato su Scarygirl, con la maggiore casa editrice indipendente australiana, Allen & Unwin. Tra le sue distinzioni spicca il Premio Aurealis 2009 per il Migliore Libro Illustrato/ Romanzo Grafico. Nel 2009 Nathan ha lanciato il gioco online Scarygirl in collaborazione con Passion Pictures Australia. Il gioco ha varcato la soglia di 1 milione di giocatori.

¿CÓMO DEFINIRÍAS TU ESTILO PERSONAL?

Arte narrativo y basado en los personajes, inspirado en la mitología y con especial énfasis en la cultura lituana.

¿QUÉ PASA POR TU MENTE CUANDO ESTÁS CREANDO UN NUEVO PERSONAJE?

Por lo general, previamente planifico mucho cómo encaja el personaje en el universo que estoy creando visualmente para ver cuáles podrían ser sus antecedentes y el modo en que interactúa con otros personajes de dicho universo.

¿CÓMO CONSEGUISTE TU PRIMER ENCARGO IMPORTANTE?

Aún estaba en la universidad, y un profesor me preguntó si me interesaría hablar sobre un proyecto con alguien de una editorial religiosa alternativa. Acabé ilustrando seis libros Infantiles para ellos

COME DEFINIRESTI IL TUO STILE PERSONALE?

Arte narrativa, animata dal carattere e ispirata al mito, con forte attenzione alla cultura lituana.

CHE COSA TI PASSA PER LA TESTA MENTRE CREI UN NUOVO PERSONAGGIO?

Generalmente c'è molta pianificazione preliminare su come il carattere si inserirà nell'universo che sto creando visualmente, su cosa potrebbe essere la storia che sta dietro e su come interagisce con gli altri caratteri in quel mondo.

COME HAI OTTENUTO LA TUA PRIMA GROSSA COMMESSA?

All'università un professore mi chiese se mi interessava un progetto con un editore religioso alternativo. Alla fine ho illustrato per loro sei libri per bambini su una nuvola volante che esplora storie antiche.

WHAT ROLE DO NEW TECHNOLOGIES PLAY IN YOUR WORK?
I'm very into games and online projects so the internet does play a large role in my work at the moment. I also work remotely so it's important to have a good art pipeline and easy access to video conferencing.

DESCRIBE YOUR IDEAL PROJECT.
I have so many ideal projects I'd like to achieve – maybe a theme park I could design from scratch based on my characters would be really fun.

par illustrer pour elle six livres qui parlaient d'un nuage volant qui explorait des histoires de l'antiquité.

QUEL RÔLE LES NOUVELLES TECHNO-LOGIES JOUENT-ELLES DANS VOTRE TRAVAIL ?
Je suis très porté sur les jeux vidéo et sur ce qui se fait en ligne, l'internet joue donc un rôle important dans ma vie en ce moment. Je travaille aussi à distance, et il est donc important d'avoir un bon flux de production artistique et un accès de qualité à la vidéoconférence.

DÉCRIVEZ VOTRE PROJET IDÉAL.
Dans l'idéal, il y a tellement de projets que j'aimerais réaliser – peut être celui d'un parc d'attraction que je dessinerais à partir de zéro et qui serait basé sur mes personnages; ce serait vraiment amusant.

sobre una nube voladora que explora historias antiguas.

¿QUÉ PAPEL DESEMPEÑAN LAS NUEVAS TECNOLOGÍAS EN TU TRABAJO?
Soy un gran aficionado a los juegos y los proyectos en línea, por lo que, en estos momentos Internet desempeña un papel muy importante en mi trabajo. Como también trabajo a distancia, es importante tener un buen flujo de producción artística y un fácil acceso a las videoconferencias.

DESCRIBE TU PROYECTO IDEAL.
Tengo tantos proyectos ideales que me gustaría hacer realidad... Poder diseñar desde cero un parque temático basado en mis personajes podría ser muy divertido.

CHE RUOLO OCCUPANO NEL TUO LAVORO LE NUOVE TECNOLOGIE?
Sono ben preso con giochi e progetti online, quindi al momento internet occupa effettivamente un ruolo importante nel mio lavoro. Per di più, lavoro spesso in remoto, quindi è importante disporre di buoni canali artistici e di un facile accesso alle videoconferenze.

DESCRIVI IL TUO PROGETTO IDEALE.
Ci sono un sacco di progetti ideali ai quali vorrei arrivare – forse un parco a tema da poter disegnare da zero in base ai miei caratteri sarebbe il più divertente.

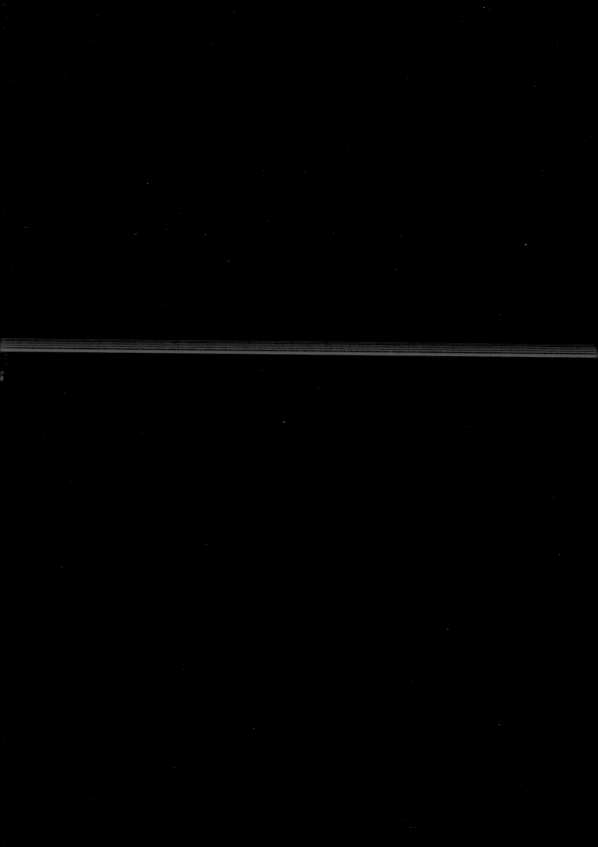

FERNANDO
FALCONE

NATHAN
JUREVICIUS

TARA
McPHERSON

MIGUEL GALLARDO

HOLA..HOLA..¿SE ME OYE?... MMMM, SOY MIGUEL GALLARDO DIBUJANTE E ILUSTRADOR... EL AUTOR DE "MARÍA Y YO", UNA NOVELA GRÁFICA SOBRE MI HIJA DE 15 AÑOS Y UN SERVIDOR EN EL MUNDO DEL RESORT...

TOC TOC

...Y AHORA ACTOR DE DOCUMENTAL (SI, YA SÉ, ES UN OXIMORÓN) EN LA PELÍCULA DEL MISMO NOMBRE...LA VERDAD ES QUE NO TENÍA NI IDEA DE QUE SE PUDIERA HACER UN DOCUMENTAL SOBRE MI LIBRO...EN REALIDAD TODO HA SIDO UN CÚMULO DE BUENAS CASUALIDADES...

FUE GRACIAS A FELIX FERNANDEZ DE TROYA, ATAMÁN DE LA PUBLICIDAD, QUE YA HABÍA LEIDO EL LIBRO Y QUE PROPUSO VAR A LA GRAN PANTALLA MI HISTORIA...

¡¡HE TENIDO UNA IDEA MÍTICA!!

¡¡¡SR. FELIX! LO LLAMAN GUCCI !!!

EL TRABAJO CON FELIX FUE MUY DURO, ES UN VERDADERO PERFECCIONISTA Y QUERÍA CAPTAR A MUERTE EL ESPÍRITU DEL LIBRO...

BARMAN, OTRO VERMÚ Y UNA FANTITA

LA VERDAD ES QUE ERA MI PRIMER PAPEL DE PROTAGONISTA Y YO ESTABA UN POCO NERVIOSO...

VAMOS ¡¡¡SAL AHI COMO UN HOMBRE Y HAZ LO QUE TIENES QUE HACER!!!

ESTAI UN POCO TENSO

¡SOY UN FIASCO!

PARA MARÍA FUE UN POCO DIFERENTE, COMO LA GRAN ESTRELLA QUE ES, LA CAMARA SE ENAMORÓ ENSEGUIDA DE ELLA...

ME ESTAIS TAPANDO EL SOL

MARÍA NO ES CONSCIENTE, CREEMOS, DE LO ABSTRACTO DE RODAR UNA PELÍCULA...

QUE NO ERA DE HABLO...

¿.. QUE ES EL NUEVO TRIO ME BAJAN LA FACTURA 20 EUROS... ER... COMO ES ESO,? ME INTERESA...

..Y .. UH ...EN QUE CONSISTE ESA...OFERTA? TENDRE MAS ANCHO DE BANDA ? ...ER... UH

POR SI NO LO HABÍA DICHO ANTES, MARÍA VIVE A 2.000 KM. DE DONDE VIVO YO, NO ES FACIL ESTAR PRESENTE Y COMUNICARSE TODAS LAS VECES QUE QUISIERA, PERO ESO SÍ, HABLAMOS CASI CADA DÍA POR TELÉFONO...

PAPI

SIEMPRE HE DICHO QUE UNA DE LAS COSAS QUE MAS NOS MOLESTAN A MI Y A LA MAYORÍA DE LOS PADRES SON LAS MIRADAS, LAS DE EXTRAÑEZA Y LAS DE LÁSTIMA, LAS DOS SON DOLOROSAS PERO LAS ÚLTIMAS INCLUYEN UNA VALORACIÓN MORAL, ESAS SÍ ME JOROBAN...

POBRECILLITA

¿SE HABRAN MIRADO ELLOS?

¡¡QUE RARA!!

MI ÚNICO CONSEJO PARA LOS PADRES QUE ESTÁN EN NUESTRA SITUACIÓN, SI ES QUE SOY ALGO PARA DAR CONSEJOS (QUE NO CREO) SON GRANDES DOSIS DE AMOR Y DE SENTIDO COMÚN...Y SOBRE TODO ESCUCHARNOS A NOSOTROS MISMOS ANTES QUE A LOS DEMÁS...

YO CREO QUE LO QUE DEBERIAIS HACER ES ...

..9 SE PRONUNCIÓ ABRA QUE... R PRONUNCIADA... EL PACK YA LE ADEMÁS ...

AGENIO

EL HORROR RETORCIÓ MIS FACCIONES...HASTA AHORA HABÍA CONSEGUIDO ESCAPAR DE LA ABOMINACIÓN...

PERO YO NO QUIERA IMAGENIO, NI SIQUIERA TENGO TELE!

PRESENTÍA UNA PRESENCIA OSCURA AL OTRO LADO DE LA LÍNEA...

PERO SEÑOR MIGUEL ANGEL, IMAGENIO ES... ¡GRATIS!

HAY MUCHA GENTE QUE ME PREGUNTA COMO ES QUE EL "PADRE DE MAKOKI" SE HA CONVERTIDO EN EL SENSIBLE "PADRE DE MARÍA" Y YO SIEMPRE LES CONTESTO QUE MARÍA HA HECHO ESTE MILAGRO, SINO, ¿QUIÉN SABE DONDE ANDARÍA YO...

DESPUES DE LA EXPERIENCIA DE RODAR ESTE DOCUMENTAL ME HE DADO CUENTA DE QUE ADEMÁS DE LA PELÍCULA EN SÍ, HEMOS HECHO ALGO IMPORTANTE...AYUDAR A LA GENTE QUE CONVIVE CON PERSONAS DIFERENTES, QUE TIENEN DIFICULTADES PARA HACER LAS COSAS MAS COTIDIANAS, ESAS PERSONAS NOS HAN DADO LAS GRACIAS POR HACER EL DOCUMENTAL...ESA ES LA RECOMPENSA MÁS BONITA QUE PODÍAMOS ESPERAR...

ER...Y...UH...AQUÍ TENGO OTRA PREGUNTA QUE LA ENVÍA UN CURA DE BADAJOZ UH...LO SIENTO, PADRE MENGANITO, PERO AHORA MISMO TENGO OTRO BOLO EN TEGUCICALPA, GRACIAS Y ABUR!!!

UNA ESPECIE DE OPIACEO ESCUCHAR LETANÍA SOBOSU...

YO ...UH SI, YO, QUE USTED QUIERA...DI

AHORA SE TORNÓE UNA SENORITA SI LE HARÍA INAS FRAGUNTAS, DU CONVERSACIÓN YA SE ACABADO PROCURE RESPONDER CON UN SI CLARETO A TODO...

ESTABA COMO HIPNOTIZADO

DE...ER...MI LLAME ASI...SOLO MIGUEL POR FAVOR...PERO YO NO QUERÍA ...UH...SI...SI...SI

BIENVENIDOS HIJOS DEL ROCANROL... A LA ERA DE ESTA CERCA

¡PAPA!

I HAVE A DREAM

UN HOMBRE, UNA MALETA, UN DESTINO...

Airbu

QUE HOSTIAS..PE..PERO SI NO HAY COLA NI NADA!

GUION

EN QUE PODEMOS SERVIRLE..SEÑOR.. SEÑOR...

40...

OH! SEÑOR GALLARDO! ESTABAMOS ESPERANDOLE..SU AVIÓN SALE EN 20 MINUTOS, PUERTA 1!

TARA McPHERSON

Tara McPherson was born in April 1976 in San Francisco, California. She currently lives and works in New York City, where she creates art about people and their idiosyncrasies. Her characters seem to exude an air of idealised innocence with a glimpse of hard-earned wisdom in their eyes. Recalling many issues from childhood and good old life experience, she creates images that are thought-provoking and seductive. People and their relationships are a central theme throughout her work.

Tara McPherson est née en avril 1976 à San Francisco en Californie. Elle vit et travaille aujourd'hui à New York, où elle crée un art qui a pour sujet les individus et leurs travers. De ses personnages semble exhaler un semblant d'innocence idéalisée avec dans leurs yeux un soupçon de lucidité durement acquise. Faisant appel à de nombreux souvenirs de son enfance et aux expériences communes de la vie, elle crée des images jugées provocantes et séduisantes. Les individus et leurs relations sont un thème central de son travail.

HOW WOULD YOU DEFINE YOUR PERSONAL STYLE?

I'd say it's a nice duality comprising the sweet and creepy, whimsical and serious, rendered and flat, light and dark. I like to focus on strange characters and their interactions with others.

HOW DID YOU FIRST GET STARTED IN THE WORLD OF ART AND/OR ILLUSTRATION?

I have always been interested in art, having gone to a Junior High and High School that specialised in art programmes. Even before I graduated from The Art Center of Pasadena, where I went to college, I had already started to do small art shows and some freelance jobs. My first big illustration job was designing four female characters for a perfume line, and I loved it. I knew I wanted more illustration jobs like that.

COMMENT DÉFINIRIEZ-VOUS VOTRE STYLE PERSONNEL ?

Je dirais que c'est un beau duel entre ce qui est doux et effrayant, fantasque et sérieux, élaboré et simple, lumineux et sombre. J'aime me concentrer sur des personnages étranges et leurs interactions avec les autres.

COMMENT AVEZ-VOUS COMMENCÉ DANS LE MONDE DE L'ART ET/OU DE L'ILLUSTRATION ?

J'ai toujours été intéressée par l'art, ayant été élève dans un collège et lycée spécialisé dans le domaine des arts. Même avant que je n'obtienne ma licence à l'Art Center de Pasadena, j'avais déjà fait de modestes expositions et travaillé en tant que freelance. Mon premier grand contrat en tant qu'illustratrice a été de dessiner quatre personnages féminins pour une ligne de parfum et j'ai adoré ça. Je savais que je voulais continuer dans ce domaine.

Tara McPherson nació en abril de 1976 en San Francisco, California. Actualmente vive y trabaja en Nueva York, donde desarrolla su labor artística, centrada en las personas y sus idiosincrasias. Aunque parece que de sus personajes emane un aire de inocencia idealizada, hay un atisbo de sabiduría ganada con esfuerzo en su mirada. Rememorando temas de su niñez y de los buenos tiempos, crea imágenes seductoras que invitan a la reflexión. Las personas y sus relaciones son un tema central en toda su obra.

Tara McPherson è nata nell'aprile del 1976 a San Francisco, California, e attualmente vive e lavora a New York, dove crea arte che parla delle persone e delle loro idiosincrasie. I suoi personaggi sembrano emanare un'aria di innocenza idealizzata, con una scintilla di saggezza guadagnata a caro prezzo nei loro occhi. Riportando alla mente varie questioni dalla gioventù e dalle care vecchie esperienze di vita, crea immagini provocanti e seduttrici. Le persone e le loro relazioni sono un tema centrale in tutte le sue opere.

¿CÓMO DEFINIRÍAS TU ESTILO PERSONAL?

Diría que es una bonita dualidad que comprende lo dulce y lo espeluznante, lo juguetón y lo serio, lo elaborado y lo sencillo, lo luminoso y lo oscuro. Me gusta centrarme en personajes extraños y en sus interacciones con los demás.

¿CÓMO TE INICIASTE EN EL MUNDO DEL ARTE Y/O LA ILUSTRACIÓN?

Siempre me ha interesado el arte porque fui a una escuela de secundaria especializada en programas de arte. Incluso antes de licenciarme del Art Center de Pasadena, ya había comenzado a hacer pequeñas exposiciones de arte y algunos trabajos como *freelance*. Mi primer trabajo importante de ilustración fue el diseño de cuatro personajes femeninos para una línea de perfumes, y me encantó. Entonces supe que quería más trabajos de ilustración como aquel.

COME DEFINIRESTI IL TUO STILE PERSONALE?

Direi che si tratta di una bella dualità tra dolce e macabro, stravagante e serio, elaborato e piatto, chiaro e scuro. Mi piace concentrarmi su strani personaggi e sulle loro interazioni con altri.

QUALI SONO STATI I TUOI INIZI NEL MONDO DELL'ARTE E/O DELL'ILLUSTRAZIONE?

Mi sono sempre interessata di arte, avendo frequentato una scuola superiore e un liceo specializzati in programmi artistici. Anche prima di laurearmi presso l'Art Center di Pasadena, il college che ho frequentato, avevo già iniziato con piccole esibizioni artistiche e lavori freelance. Il primo grosso lavoro di illustrazione è stato il disegno di quattro personaggi femminili per una linea di profumi, e mi è piaciuto davvero. Dopo quel lavoro, sapevo che ne avrei voluti altri.

WHAT LED YOU TO START CREATING CHARACTERS?

Well, I had always loved character-driven art, but it was my experience running a Japanese animation and toy shop before college that solidified this vocation. It was then I knew that I wanted to do the same things... create my own characters, make toys, and make art that supported a world of situations that I could create and explore. That's when I finally decided to go to art school (instead of becoming a tattoo artist) and really learn how to paint and draw.

WHAT GOES THROUGH YOUR MIND WHEN YOU ARE CREATING A NEW CHARACTER?

Excitement goes through my mind! It's the birth of a new "life"! I end up creating the best characters when I'm just doodling. Sometimes one idea looks cooler than the other and you think to yourself, "this little guy has something"! Then you name it, and it becomes part of the gang. And I like to refine the character over time as well, redrawing to define its look and features.

DESCRIBE YOUR IDEAL PROJECT.

One with no art directors telling me what to do! Well not really, I actually love great art direction, but I truly work best when I'm allowed the freedom to create whatever I feel inclined to create. Without limitations.

QU'EST-CE QUI VOUS A AMENÉ À CRÉER DES PERSONNAGES?

Eh bien, j'ai toujours aimé l'art axé sur des personnages mais c'est mon expérience en tant que gérante d'une boutique d'animés et de *toys* japonais avant l'université qui a consolidé cette vocation. C'est alors que j'ai su que je voulais faire la même chose... créer mes propres personnages, en faire des *toys*, et proposer un art qui offre un monde de situations que je pouvais créer et explorer. C'est ce qui m'a enfin décidé à m'inscrire dans une école d'art (plutôt que de devenir une artiste en tatouage) et y apprendre vraiment à peindre et à dessiner.

A QUOI PENSEZ-VOUS QUAND VOUS CRÉEZ UN NOUVEAU PERSONNAGE ?

Mon esprit est en ébullition ! C'est la naissance d'une "vie" nouvelle. Je finis par créer les meilleurs personnages quand je suis juste en train de griffonner. Parfois une idée vous semble plus chouette qu'une autre et vous vous dites, "ce petit bonhomme a quelque chose !". Et puis vous lui donnez un nom et il devient un membre de la bande. Et j'aime peaufiner le personnage au fil du temps en redessinant son apparence et ses traits.

DÉCRIVEZ VOTRE PROJET IDÉAL.

Un projet sans directeur artistique qui me dise quoi faire ! Enfin pas vraiment, car, en fait, j'aime une bonne direction artistique, mais je travaille vraiment bien mieux quand on me laisse la liberté de créer ce que je suis encline à faire. Sans aucune limite.

¿QUÉ TE LLEVÓ A COMENZAR A CREAR PERSONAJES?

Bueno, siempre me había gustado el arte que se basa en los personajes, pero esta vocación se consolidó antes de ir a la universidad cuando trabajé dirigiendo una tienda de *toys* y animación japonesa. Fue entonces cuando supe que quería hacer lo mismo: crear mis propios personajes, hacer *toys* y producir un tipo de arte que secundara un mundo de situaciones que pudiera crear y explorar. Fue entonces cuando finalmente decidí ir a la facultad de bellas artes —en lugar de convertirme en una artista tatuadora— a aprender a pintar y dibujar de verdad.

¿EN QUÉ PIENSAS CUANDO ESTÁS CREANDO UN NUEVO PERSONAJE?

¡La emoción! ¡Se trata del nacimiento de una nueva "vida"! Acabo creando los mejores personajes cuando estoy haciendo garabatos. A veces una idea parece más chula que otra, y piensas: "¡Este pequeñuelo tiene algo!". Entonces le das un nombre, y se convierte en uno más de la pandilla. También me gusta ir puliendo el personaje con el tiempo, volviéndolo a dibujar para definir su aspecto y sus características.

DESCRIBE TU PROYECTO IDEAL.

¡Uno en que no haya directores de arte diciéndome lo que he de hacer! Bueno, en realidad no, ya que de hecho me encanta la buena dirección de arte, pero lo cierto es que cuando mejor trabajo es cuando tengo libertad para hacer lo que sea que me apetezca crear. Sin limitaciones.

CHE COSA TI HA PORTATO A INIZIARE A CREARE PERSONAGGI?

Diciamo che ho sempre amato l'arte basata su personaggi, ma questa vocazione è stata consolidata dall'esperienza di gestire un negozio di animazione e *toys* giapponesi prima dell'università. A quel punto seppi che volevo fare le stesse cose... creare i miei personaggi, ideare *toys* e creare arte che supportasse un mondo di situazioni che potessi creare ed esplorare. A quel punto ho deciso di prendere la strada della scuola d'arte (invece di diventare una tattoo artist) e imparare davvero a disegnare e dipingere.

CHE COSA TI PASSA PER LA TESTA MENTRE CREI UN NUOVO PERSONAGGIO?

Eccitazione è quello che mi passa per la testa! È la nascita di una nuova "vita"! Alla fine creo i personaggi migliori da semplici scarabocchi. A volte un'idea sembra più *cool* di un'altra e ti dici, "questo piccoletto ha qualcosa"! Poi gli dai un nome e diventa parte della banda. Mi piace anche raffinare il personaggio con l'andare del tempo e ridisegnarlo per definire il suo *look* e le sue caratteristiche.

DESCRIVI IL TUO PROGETTO IDEALE.

Uno senza direttori artistici che mi dicano cosa fare! Beh, non proprio... a dire il vero adoro una buona direzione artistica, ma lavoro al meglio quando ho la libertà di creare qualsiasi cosa mi senta portata a creare. Senza limiti.

Having studied at Barcelona's Massana School, Miguel Gallardo started his career combining comics – he was one of the creators of Makoki, an iconic underground character – with illustration. His illustrations regularly grace national and international newspapers such as *La Vanguardia, El Público and the International Herald Tribune*. He designs book covers for the top Spanish publishing houses. He has won several awards, including notably from the Barcelona Comic Convention, the Society of Newspaper Design, the APIC and, in 2008, a Catalan Government National Prize in the comic category, as well as various prizes for his graphic novel *María y yo*.

Après avoir étudié à l'École Massana de Barcelone, il commence sa carrière en mélangeant la bande dessinée - il est l'un des auteurs de Makoki, célèbre icône *underground* - et l'illustration. Il collabore régulièrement, comme illustrateur de presse nationale et internationale pour *La Vanguardia, El Público* et *l'International Herald Tribune*, entre autres. Il réalise la couverture de livres d'importants éditeurs espagnols et a remporté plusieurs récompenses dont celle du Salon de la bande dessinée de Barcelone, de la Society of Newspaper Design, de l'APIC et le Prix National de la Generalitat dans la catégorie du Comic en 2008, ainsi que plusieurs prix pour son roman graphique *Maria y Yo*.

HOW WOULD YOU DEFINE YOUR PERSONAL STYLE?

My personal style is the lack of a defined style. In other words, my style changes depending on the subject I have to illustrate, the format, my mood and whether I've slept well or not. Basically, I see my work as a game in which rather than playing by other people's rules, I make my own.

HOW DO YOU GO ABOUT CREATING A NEW CHARACTER? WHAT GOES THROUGH YOUR MIND?

The truth is that it wasn't too much of a stretch for me to come up with my most recent characters: for *Un largo silencio*, I drew my inspiration from my father and his experiences during the Civil War, for which he was on the losing side, and his subsequent ordeals at various French concentration camps; it is a tale of the defeated. In *María y yo*, a diary of a

COMMENT DÉFINIRIEZ-VOUS VOTRE STYLE ?

Mon style personnel est l'absence d'un style particulier. En d'autres termes mon style change en fonction du sujet que je dois illustrer, du format, de mon état d'esprit et si j'ai bien ou mal dormi. En gros, je vois mon travail comme un jeu dans lequel, au lieu de suivre les règles des autres, je crée mes propres règles.

COMMENT PROCÉDEZ-VOU QUAND VOUS CRÉEZ UN NOUVEAU PERSONNAGE? QU'AVEZ-VOUS EN TÊTE ?

En vérité, créer mes tout derniers personnages ne m'a pas demandé beaucoup d'effort d'imagination : pour *Un largo silencio*, je me suis inspiré de mon père et de son expérience lors de la guerre civile, de la défaite, car il était du côté des perdants et des épreuves dans les camps de concentration français. C'est un récit des perdants. Dans *Maria y yo*, un journal

Estudió en la Escuela Massana de Barcelona. Comenzó su carrera profesional compaginando el cómic —fue uno de los autores de Makoki, personaje icono del *underground*— con la ilustración. Colabora habitualmente como ilustrador de prensa nacional e internacional en *La Vanguardia*, *El Público* y el *International Herald Tribune*, entre otros y realiza portadas para las principales editoriales españolas. Ha ganado varios premios entre los que destacan el del Salón del Cómic, la Society of Newspaper Design, un premio de prensa del APIC y el Premi Nacional de la Generalitat 2008 en la categoría de cómic, así como otros premios por su novela gráfica *María y yo*.

¿CÓMO DEFINIRÍAS TU ESTILO PERSONAL?

Mi estilo personal es el no estilo. Este cambia en función del tema que tenga que ilustrar, del soporte, de mi estado de ánimo y de si he dormido bien o no. Básicamente, concibo mi trabajo como un juego en el que empleo mis propias reglas y no las de los demás.

¿EN QUÉ TE BASAS A LA HORA DE CREAR UN NUEVO PERSONAJE? ¿QUÉ PASA POR TU CABEZA?

La verdad es que los últimos personajes en los que he trabajado no han necesitado de mucha imaginación: para *Un largo silencio*, mi padre y su experiencia en la guerra civil, la derrota y su internamiento en los campos de concentración franceses; se trata de una crónica de perdedores. En *María y yo*, un diario de vacaciones con mi hija María de 14 años y con Trastorno del Espectro Autista,

Dopo gli studi alla Escuela Massana di Barcellona, ha iniziato la sua carriera professionale alternando il fumetto – è uno degli autori di Makoki, personaggio icona dell'underground – con l'illustrazione. Collabora regolarmente come illustratore per la stampa nazionale e internazionale su *La Vanguardia*, *El Público* e l'*International Herald Tribune*, tra gli altri, e si occupa di copertine per le principali case editrici spagnole. Si è aggiudicato vari premi, tra i quali spiccano il Salone del Fumetto, la Società del Disegno per Quotidiani, un premio per la stampa dell'APIC e il Premio Nazionale del Governo della Catalogna 2008 nella categoria del fumetto, oltre ad altri premi per il suo romanzo grafico *María y yo*.

COME DEFINIRESTI IL TUO STILE PERSONALE?

Il mio stile personale è il non-stile, che varia in funzione dell'argomento da illustrare, del formato, dello stato d'animo e del fatto di avere dormito bene o no. Fondamentalmente concepisco il mio lavoro come un gioco nel quale valgono le mie regole e non quelle altrui.

SU COSA TI BASI AL MOMENTO DI CREARE UN NUOVO PERSONAGGIO? CHE COSA TI PASSA PER LA TESTA?

A dire il vero, gli ultimi personaggi sui quali ho lavorato non hanno avuto bisogno di molta immaginazione: per *Un largo silencio*, mio padre e la sua esperienza nella guerra civile e nella sconfitta con successiva prigionia nei campi di concentrazione francesi: una cronaca di sconfitti. In *María y yo*, un diario delle vacanze con mia figlia María, di 14 anni, che soffre di disturbo di tipo autistico, il personaggio —lei stessa— non richiede molta

holiday with my 14-year-old daughter, María, who has an Autism Spectrum Disorder, the character – María herself – did not require much imagination; she's got enough off the stuff for the rest of us put together. And finally, in a lot of my comics the main character is based on myself, in various particular guises, ranging from the millionaire illustrator to the simpleton who misses the bus and loses his ID card.

HAVE YOU EVER FELT INHIBITED WHEN CREATING A NEW STORY OUT OF FEAR OF BEING CENSORED OR PEOPLE DISLIKING YOUR WORK?
Only in the case of newspapers which already operate a sort of internalised censorship with regards to so-called taboo subjects like sex or the king.

WHAT'S THE SECRET TO THE SUCCESS OF YOUR CHARACTERS/STORIES?
I think it's the fact that the characters, and most of the stories, are based on real people and events, combined with 20 years' experience as a humorist and clown, which allow me to distance myself from things sufficiently so as to make any subject approachable and fun.

DESCRIBE YOUR PERSONAL PROJECT.
My personal project is an account of a trip to Tokyo during which my daughter María and I walk down the street and people turn their heads and say "That's María, she's something special".

de vacances avec ma fille Maria, âgée de 14 ans et atteinte de troubles du spectre autistique, le personnage – Maria elle-même – n'a pas demandé beaucoup d'effort d'imagination ; elle en a plus que nous tous réunis. Et enfin, dans beaucoup de mes histoires, le personnage est basé sur moi-même, sous des apparences variées, de l'illustrateur millionnaire au nigaud qui rate son bus et perd sa carte d'identité.

VOUS ÊTES-VOUS DÉJÀ SENTI INHIBÉ QUAND VOUS CRÉEZ UNE NOUVELLE HISTOIRE PAR PEUR DE LA CENSURE OU PAR PEUR DE DÉPLAIRE ?
Seulement en ce qui concerne les journaux qui opèrent leur propre censure quant aux sujets tabous comme le sexe ou le roi.

QUELLE EST LA CLÉ DU SUCCÈS DE VOS PERSONNAGES ET HISTOIRES?
Je crois que c'est dû au fait que mes personnages et la plupart de mes histoires sont basés sur des personnes ou des faits réels. A cela s'ajoutent mes 20 années d'expérience en tant qu'humoriste et clown qui m'ont permis de prendre suffisamment de distance afin de rendre accessibles et amusants les thèmes traités.

DÉCRIVEZ VOTRE PROJET PERSONNEL.
Mon projet personnel est un récit d'un voyage à Tokyo durant lequel Maria et moi marchons dans la rue et les gens se retournent sur nous en disant : « C'est Maria, c'est quelqu'un de spécial. »

el personaje —ella misma— no precisa mucha imaginación; ella la tiene por todos los demás. Y por último, el personaje que he utilizado en mis últimas historietas soy yo mismo, en unas caracterizaciones particulares que van desde el ilustrador millonario al inútil que pierde el autobús y el carnet de identidad.

¿ALGUNA VEZ TE HAS SENTIDO COARTADO A LA HORA DE CREAR UNA NUEVA HISTORIA POR TEMOR A QUE TE CENSURARAN O TE DIJERAN QUE NO LES GUSTABA TU OBRA?
Solo en los periódicos en los que ya rige una censura interiorizada con respecto a temas tabú como el sexo o el rey.

¿CUÁL ES LA CLAVE DEL ÉXITO DE TUS PERSONAJES Y TUS HISTORIAS?
Creo que es el hecho de que los personajes estén basados en personas de verdad y de que casi todas las historias sean reales, unido a 20 años de humorista y payaso que me dan el suficiente distanciamiento de las cosas como para hacer legible y divertido cualquier tema.

DESCRIBE TU PROYECTO PERSONAL.
Mi proyecto personal es un diario sobre mi viaje a Tokio y que cuando mi hija María y yo vayamos por la calle, la gente gire la cabeza y diga: "Esa es María, es alguien especial".

immaginazione: lei ne ha abbastanza per tutti. Infine, il personaggio che ho utilizzato nelle mie ultime strisce sono io stesso, in caratterizzazioni particolari, dall'illustratore milionario all'incapace che perde l'autobus e la carta d'identità.

IN QUALE OCCASIONE TI SEI SENTITO LIMITATO AL MOMENTO DI CREARE UNA NUOVA STORIA PER PAURA DELLA CENSURA, O DI SENTIRTI DIRE CHE LA TUA OPERA NON PIACEVA?
Solo nei quotidiani nei quali vige una censura interna determinata riguardo ad argomenti tabù, come il sesso o il re.

QUAL È LA CHIAVE DEL SUCCESSO DEI TUOI PERSONAGGI E DELLE TUE STORIE.
Credo che sia il fatto che i personaggi si basano su persone in carne e ossa e che quasi tutte le mie storie sono reali, uniti ai 20 anni come umorista e pagliaccio che mi permettono un distacco dalle cose sufficiente a rendere leggibile e divertente qualsiasi argomento.

DESCRIVI IL TUO PROGETTO IDEALE.
Il mio progetto personale è un diario sul mio viaggio a Tokyo e che quando mia figlia María e io camminiamo per strada la gente si giri e dica: "Quella è María, una persona speciale".

AGENTEMORILLAS
P. 102, 107, 129, 178

info@agentemorillas.com
www.agentemorillas.com
elblogdeagentemorillas.blogspot.com
Barcelona (ES)

AGU MÉNDEZ
P. 34, 60, 120, 128

agu@pensamientosdeformados.com
www.pensamientosdeformados.com
Málaga (ES)

AGUSTÍN VIGUERA
P. 24, 57, 106

ruidismo@gmail.com
www.ruidismo.com
Buenos Aires (AR)

AIIKO VOLSY
P. 11, 87

aurelie_volsy@yahoo.fr
aiiko.blogspot.com
Barcelona (ES)

ALICIA VARELA CASO
P. 50, 56

alicia@aliciavarela.es
www.aliciavarela.es
Gijón (ES)

ANDRÉS RODRÍGUEZ
P. 134, 180

www.androp.cl
Santiago de Chile (CL)

ANNA FONT
P. 31, 68, 121, 132

annafont73@gmail.com
www.annafont.blogspot.com
Barcelona (ES)

ARIAN [ZAL] NOVEIR
P. 144

arian.noveir@gmail.com
www.noveir.com
Ris Orangis (FR)

ARNAUD BOUTIN
P. 104

contact@arnaudboutin.com
www.arnaudboutin.com
arnaudboutin.blogspot.com
Paris (FR)

ASHER B. EGGLESTON
P. 192, 193

asher@mindsize.us
www.mindsize.us
www.asher-eggleston.blogspot.com
Rhode Island (US)

AYAKO OKUBO
P. 62, 155, 164

kitekiss@me.com
web.me.com/kitekiss
Tokyo (JP)

BROSMIND (ALEJANDRO & JUAN MINGARRO)
P. 26, 69, 125

info@brosmind.com
www.brosmind.com
Barcelona (ES)

CHRISTIAN VOLTZ
P. 13, 41, 47

christian@christianvoltz.com
www.christianvoltz.com
Strasbourg (FR)

CLÉMENCE KERTUDO
P. 39, 58, 119, 123

clemencekertu@gmail.com
klem-graphik.blogspot.com
Barcelona (ES)

DAMIÁN CONCI
P. 76, 142

damian@concimelnizki.com.ar
concimelnizki.com.ar
Buenos Aires (AR)

DAN MATUTINA
P. 25, 91, 98

psst@twistedfork.me
twistedfork.me
twistedfork.tumblr.com
Quezon City (PH)

DANIEL DÍAZ PIÑEIRO
P. 60

daniel.dipi@gmail.com
daniel--pinheiro.blogspot.com
Berlin (DE)

DIANE KOSS – CUTESY BUT NOT CUTESY
P. 22, 103, 109, 111

dkoss2@gmail.com
www.cutesybutnotcutesy.com
dkoss2.blogspot.com
Philadelphia (US)

EGGPINIC (CAMILA DE GREGORIO & CHRISTOPHER MACALUSO)
P. 109, 134

Camila De Gregorio &
Christopher Macaluso
hello@eggpicnic.com
www.eggpicnic.com
Santiago de Chile (CL)

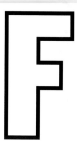

FABRICE LE NEZET
P. 198, 199

f.lenezet@gmail.com
London (GB)

FEDERICO ORRÚ
P. 177

gliamicidelbosco@gmail.com
Barcelona (ES)

FERNANDO FALCONE
P. 203, 204, 205, 206, 207, 215

mail@fernandofalcone.com.ar
www.fernandofalcone.com.ar
Buenos Aires (AR)

FRAN FERRIZ
P. 65, 94, 96, 139

fcoferriz@gmail.com
www.franferriz.com
franferriz.blogspot.com
Villena (ES)

FRANCISCO ALBERT ALBUSAC
P. 194, 195

Francis.jaa@gmail.com
Úbeda (ES)

FRANK PLANT
P. 10, 130

www.frankplant.net
Barcelona (ES)

GENEVIÈVE GAUCKLER
P. 20, 21, 59, 105, 146, 147, 168,

genevievegauckler@me.com
www.genevievegauckler.com
Paris (FR)

GÉRALDINE COSNEAU
P. 57, 132

cosmos.chocolat@yahoo.fr
geraldine-cosneau.blogspot.com
Nantes (FR)

GHOSTPATROL
P. 78

www.ghostpatrol.net
Melbourne (AU)

GILLES FRELUCHE
P. 95, 96

aka Soyouzgraphic
gilles@soyouzgraphic.com
www.soyouzgraphic.com
Barcelona (ES)

GINA THORSTENSEN
P. 37, 102, 131, 156, 157

ginathorstensen@gmail.com
www.ginathorstensen.com
Copenhagen (DK)

GREG. " LEON " GUILLEMIN
P. 80, 87, 172

greg.guillemin@orange.fr
www.greg-guillemin.com
Rochefort-en-Yvelines (FR)

GRELIN MACHIN
P. 89, 97, 99

grelinmachin@gmail.com
grelinmachin.artworkfolio.com
Montreal (CA)

**GUADALUPE LABAKÉ
& NICOLÁS SÁNCHEZ**
P. 186, 187

guadalabake@yahoo.com
Buenos Aires (AR)

**GUILLAUME
PAIN -TOUGUI**
P. 114, 135

touguidzn@gmail.com
www.tougui.fr
touguil.blogspot.com
Paris (FR)

GUY BLOOM
P. 181

gay.bloom@gmail.com
www.diozart.com
Barcelona (ES)

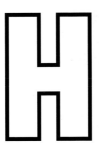

HAPPYMIAOW
P. 14, 33, 174

happymiaow@gmail.com
www.happymiaow.es
Barcelona (ES)

HARUKA SHINJI
P. 18, 180

haruka@harukashinji.com
www.harukashinji.com
Tokyo (JP)

HEDOF - RICK BERKELMANS
P. 71, 84

rickb@hedof.nl
www.hedof.nl
Breda (NL)

HELENA GARCIA
P. 55, 56, 100

helena@helenagarcia.com
www.helenagarcia.com
Florida (US)

ILU·STATION
P. 4, 5, 6, 7

hola@ilustation.com
www.mini-station.blogspot.com
www.ilustation.com
Barcelona (ES)

ISIDRO FERRER
P. 28, 32, 41, 44

isidroferrer@telefonica.net
www.isidroferrer.com
Huesca (ES)

JAVI MEDIALDEA
P. 179

javi@medialdea.net
www.medialdea.net
Málaga (ES)

JEAN JULLIEN
P. 128, 159

jean.jullien@gmail.com
www.jeanjullien.com
London (GB)

JIM WHITTAMORE
P. 133

www.jimbobbin.com
Brighton (GB)

JOANNA ZHOU
P. 52, 161

www.chocolatepixels.com
Viena (AT)

JOÃO LAURO FONTE
P. 40, 90

www.laurofonte.com
www.laurofonteblog.
wordpress.com
London (GB)

JOAQUÍN ALDEGUER
P. 176, 196, 197

j.aldeguer@gmail.com
joaquinaldeguer.blogspot.com
Alicante (ES)

JUAN PABLO CAMBARIERE
P. 42, 43

jp@cambariere.com
www.cambariere.com
Buenos Aires (AR)

KEITA TAKAHASHI
P. 33, 52

www.uvula.jp
Tokyo (JP)

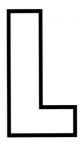

LA PRINCESITA
P. 58, 140

laprincesita@princesitastyle.com
www.princesitastyle.com
meriprincesita.blogspot.com
Málaga (ES)

LEÓN KITAY
P. 19

leo.kitay@axisdisenio.com.ar
uncuartitodepaz.com.ar
Buenos Aires (AR)

LHWOLF
P. 182, 183

lhwolfbr@gmail.com
www.lhwolf.com
Barcelona (ES)

MACN
P. 29, 30

martin.cocchi@gmail.com
www.macnmacn.com
Buenos Aires (AR)

MALICIA
P. 150, 151

maliciawalls@gmail.com
Barcelona (ES)

MARK GMEHLING
P. 12, 48, 88, 108

mark.gmehling@braincorps.de
www.markgmehling.weebly.com
Dortmund (DE)

MARTIN HSU
P. 126

info@martinhsu.com
www.martinhsu.com
San Francisco (US)

MICHELA AIMI
P. 73

michekat@libero.it
Dublin (IE)

MICRO.BARBI
P. 27, 160

micro.barbi@gmail.com
www.micro.barbi.blogspot.com
Barcelona (ES)

MIGUEL GALLARDO
P. 218, 227, 228, 229, 230, 231

www.miguel-gallardo.com
Barcelona (ES)

MIKEL CASAL
P. 113, 154

ilustracion@mikelcasal.com
www.mikelcasal.com
San Sebastián (ES)

MIZNA WADA
P. 54, 83, 179

mizna@hihou.net
www.hihou.net/mizna
Kumamoto (JP)

MUTTO (GUILLE MUÑOZ)
P. 146

mail@mutto.com.ar
www.mutto.com.ar
mutto.com.ar/blog
Buenos Aires (AR)

NAOSHI
P. 63, 103

sunae@nao-shi.com
www.nao-shi.com
Yokohama (JP)

NATHAN JUREVICIUS
P. 209, 210, 211, 212, 213, 216

www.scarygirl.com
www.nathanj.com.au
Toronto (CA)

NICOLÁS NAZARENO SARSOTTI
P. 17, 34, 81

nicosarso@yahoo.com.ar
Buenos Aires (AR)

NUMI MIDORI
P. 16, 52, 62,

hellonumi@gmail.com
www.missnumi.net
Seoul (KR)

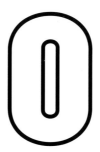

ORNE CABRITA
P. 82, 92

contact@ocabrita.com
www.ocabrita.com
www.ocabrita.blogspot.com
Barcelona (ES)

OSCAR CHÁVEZ
P. 66, 67, 82, 127

chavezonico@gmail.com
www.chavezonico.com
Santiago de Chile (CL)

PARQUERAMA STUDIOS
P. 183

hello@parqueramastudios.tv
www.parqueramastudios.tv
Buenos Aires (AR)

PASCAL VALDES
P. 35, 57, 163

pascalvaldes@free.fr
pascalvaldes.free.fr
Paris (FR)

PAULA CELINA RAMOS
P. 190, 191

ilusiones_design@hotmail.com
paulailustraciones.blogspot.com
Buenos Aires (AR)

PERRY DIXON MAPLE
P. 67, 68, 91, 188, 189

perry.maple@designu4ia.com
California (US)

PEZ
P. 148

www.el-pez.com
Bogotá (CO)

RED NOSE STUDIO
P. 72, 75, 136, 137

art@magnetreps.com
www.magnetreps.com
Indiana (US)

RICCARDO ZEMA
P. 36, 38, 45

bug3d@hotmail.com
www.kidqube.com
Faenza (IT)

RILLA ALEXANDER
P. 166

rilla@byrilla.com
www.byrilla.com
www.sozi.com
Berlin (DE)

RORY MITCHELL
P. 85, 107, 114, 158

rory80@gmail.com
www.rorymitchell.co.uk
London (GB)

RUMPUS ANIMATION
P. 136

joe@rumpusanimation.com
www.rumpusanimation.com
rumpusfilm.blogspot.com
Bristol (GB)

RYAN CHAPMAN
P. 15, 70, 175

ryan-chapman@hotmail.com
www.ryan-chapman.com
Melbourne (AU)

 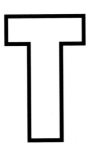    

INDEX OF ARTISTS ON CD

YING YANG
Ana Muñoz Guerrero
anuska_617@hotmail.com
Málaga (ES)

BAILARINA
Carolina Varas Bueno
cvaras298@gmail.com
Pamplona (ES)

PELICAN
Guillem Bosch
guillem75@hotmail.com
guillemdaki.blogspot.com
Barcelona (ES)

BANJO
Guy Bloom
gay.bloom@gmail.com
www.diozart.com
Barcelona (ES)

DISCOS DUROS
Carmen Jiménez
ca_mi_ve@hotmail.com
dorcarmenjimenez.blogspot.com
Córdoba (ES)

BORC
Daniel Crespo Boquera
dcrespoboquera@gmail.com
Barcelona (ES)

NIKITO
Daniel Díaz Piñeiro
daniel.dipi@gmail.com
www.danieldiazpinheiro.blogspot.com
Berlin (DE)

DRAGUI
Jose Manuel
Cepeda García
Sevilla (ES)

**CÁPSULAS
PARA EL RESFRIADO**
Laura Sánchez Ternero
laezne@gmail.com
Málaga (ES)

HIPSTBIRD
María Gratsia
maria.gratsia@gmail.com
Barcelona (ES)

ANNIE
Pilar Martín
pilar.ml87@gmail.com
Benamejí (ES)

TAR-LASS
Venus Müler Capdevila
alegria_fxs@hotmail.com
Barcelona (ES)

**MUÑECAS
MELANCÓLICAS**
Lidia Matas
yopaso@hotmail.com
Granada (ES)

HEY SAILOR!
Rafa Sánchez
rafasanchezgil@gmail.com
amordepixel.blospot.com
Málaga (ES)

BUBA
Renata Ortega
renadisseny@gmail.com
www.laranabcn.com
renadisseny.blogspot.com
Terrassa (ES)

**ART CÚBIC
ESCOLA**
Sant Frederic 56
08028 Barcelona (ES)
escola@artcubic.net
www.artcubic.net

**BAU,
ESCUELA SUPERIOR
DE DISEÑO**
Pujades 118
08005 Barcelona (ES)
info@bau.cat
www.baued.es

**GAUSS MULTIMEDIA
ESCUELA DE DISEÑO**
Avenida Plutarco, 75, local 12.
Teatinos
29010 Málaga (ES)
info@gaussmultimedia.com

PHOTO CREDITS

© **Bruño:** Floristela, Merlimberto y Patinete. (Tesa González)
© **Dolly Oblong:** Paper Totem! (Tuomas Ikonen)
© **Downtown Nassau Partnership:** Hello Nassau. (Thundercut)
© **Edelvives:** Goss. (Tesa González)
© **Edelbé:** Rey grande. (Tesa González)
© **Fernando Alvira:** Flamenco. (Isidro Ferrer)
© **Fred & Ginger – Zeptonn:** Business characters. (Zeptonn)
© **El circo de la publicidad, S.L.:** Godzilla, Rikishi.(Javi Medialdea)
© **Jacinto Esteban:** Elefante. (Isidro Ferrer)
© **Jeff Ragovin:** Rumpus New York. (Rumpus animation)
© **Jekyll et Hyde:** Hábitos alimenticios. (Zosen)
© **Jon Compton:** Cutesy Monster Mascot. (Diane Koss)
© **Kaching Brands & Mizna Wada:** Lollipop girl. (Mizna Wada)
© **Kazuo Fukunaga & Takashi Hinoda:** Deprivation of the throne, Zombie brothers, The world. (Takashi Hinoda)
© **Mago Production, TV3:** Dr. W. (Andrés Rodriguez)
© **Meritxell Arjalaguer:** Brosmind Army, Larry, Norman. (Brosmind)
© **Michel Lagarde:** Mon premier jour de classe. (Arnaud Boutin)
© **Pinka Productions:** Garage Club – The neighbours & The backing singer. (Pascal Valdes)
© **Shogakukan & Mizna Wada:** Zigokku Enma. (Mizna Wada)
© **Steven Emmanuel:** Family. (Jean Jullien)
© **Toy2R:** Rolitoboy, Kid 666, A mixed shot of 2.5" Qees, 3.5" Baby Qee - Lunna Edition, 2.5" 1000th Qee - Clear Boxee Head.
© **Tsukasa Yunoue & Ayako Okubo:** Commanders in the last East. (Ayako Okubo)
© **Xavier d'Arquer:** El cabolo cuiner. (Isidro Ferrer)

ILU·STATION
Mini-Station logo
Mascot contest 2010
Paper table football
Ilu·Station workshop logo
Ilu·Station Christmas poster 2009
Ilu·Station workshop set-up

FERNANDO FALCONE
Abrazo (La comunidad - Agencia de publicidad)
Almuerzo
Dama duende (Ediciones Parramón)
El sueño del conejo
La estrella (Revista Bglam)
Tecno (Revista Terrorismo gráfico)

NATHAN JUREVICIUS
Tree of knowledge
Swampfolk
Dievasw
Ring around the queen
Harlow

TARA McPHERSON
Laughing through the chaos of it all
Hey we all die sometimes
The dull sound
A halloween portrait
Lost constellations
The love space is as deep as the oceans

MIGUEL GALLARDO
Me, myself
María y yo, the movie
María y yo
I have a dream
El horror de Dunwich